THE PEACE OF THE CHURCH

By the same Author.

———◆———

THE CHURCH IDEA. An Essay
towards Unity.

CONDITIONAL IMMORTALITY.
[Out of print.]

THE CAUSES OF THE SOUL.
A Book of Sermons.

The Bohlen Lectures for 1891

THE

PEACE OF THE CHURCH

BY

WILLIAM REED HUNTINGTON

RECTOR OF GRACE CHURCH NEW YORK

In Veritate Victoria

New York

CHARLES SCRIBNER'S SONS

1891

260
H 926

Copyright, 1891, by
WILLIAM REED HUNTINGTON.

𝔘niversity 𝔓ress:
JOHN WILSON AND SON, CAMBRIDGE.

TO

THE DEAR MEMORY OF

H. H.

WHO ALIKE BY PRECEPT AND BY EXAMPLE

TAUGHT ME HOPE.

THE JOHN BOHLEN LECTURESHIP.

JOHN BOHLEN, who died in this city on the twenty-sixth day of April, 1874, bequeathed to trustees a fund of One Hundred Thousand Dollars, to be distributed to religious and charitable objects in accordance with the well-known wishes of the testator.

By a deed of trust, executed June 2, 1875, the trustees, under the will of Mr. BOHLEN, transferred and paid over to "The Rector, Church Wardens, and Vestrymen of the Church of the Holy Trinity, Philadelphia," in trust, a sum of money for certain designated purposes, out of which fund the sum of Ten Thousand Dollars was set apart for the endowment of THE JOHN BOHLEN LECTURESHIP, upon the following terms and conditions : —

"The money shall be invested in good, substantial, and safe securities, and held in trust for a fund to be called The John Bohlen Lectureship; and the income shall be applied annually to the payment of a qualified person, whether clergyman or layman, for the delivery and publication of at least one hundred copies of two or more lecture sermons. These lectures shall be delivered at such time and place, in the city of Philadelphia, as the persons nominated to appoint the lecturer shall from time to time determine, giving at least six months' notice to the person appointed to deliver the same, when the same may conveniently be done, and in no case selecting the same person as lecturer a second time within a period of five years. The payment shall be made to said lecturer, after the lectures have been printed, and received by the trustees, of all the income for the year derived from said fund, after defraying the expense of printing the lectures, and the other incidental expenses attending the same.

"The subject of such lectures shall be such as is within the terms set forth in the will of the Rev. John Bampton, for the delivery of what are known as the 'Bampton Lectures,' at Oxford, or any other subject distinctively connected with or relating to the Christian religion.

"The lecturer shall be appointed annually in the month of May, or as soon thereafter as can conveniently be done, by the persons who for the time being shall hold the offices of Bishop of the Protestant Episcopal Church of the Diocese in which is the Church of the Holy Trinity; the Rector of said Church; the Professor of Biblical Learning, the Professor of Systematic Divinity, and the Professor of Ecclesiastical History, in the Divinity School of the Protestant Episcopal Church in Philadelphia.

"In case either of said offices are vacant, the others may nominate the lecturer."

Under this trust the Reverend William R. Huntington, D.D., D.C.L., Rector of Grace Church, New York, was appointed to deliver the lectures for the Year 1891.

PHILADELPHIA, EASTER, 1891,

**THE WANT OF A PEOPLE'S CHURCH IS A WANT THAT
CANNOT BE SUPPLIED BY ANYTHING ELSE.**

VON DÖLLINGER.

PREFACE.

————◆————

A NATURAL comment upon the general drift of argument and appeal in the following pages would be that it is too conspicuously Protestant. Are the children of the Reformation, the author might very plausibly be asked, the only Christian folk to be counted in forecasting the contour and proportions of our national Church? Is no significance to be attached to the marvellous growth and spread among us of the Latin form of Christ's religion in these recent days? And have we no word of invitation for those who differ with us in their estimate of the value of the results Luther and Cranmer brought to pass? Certainly there is force in these expostulations. To wink the advance of Roman Catholic religion in this country out of sight is as foolish as the letting ourselves be irritated by what we see is weak.

Neither are those to be commended who can see in the activity of the Papal forces nothing less or other than a distinct menace to our civilization. The real reason why the conciliatory effort of this book bends wholly towards a different point of the

compass is that, for the present, any attempt from
without to influence the Roman Catholic Church is
absolutely hopeless. The Vatican decrees of 1870
have accomplished what the framers and promoters
of them doubtless meant that they should accomplish, — the utter overthrow of any hopes of "peace
with Rome" on ground other than that of unconditional surrender. Meanwhile there is much to encourage the belief that, in ways hidden from the eyes
of outsiders, a change is going on within the confines
of the Roman Church in this country, likely, at no
very distant day, to become knowable and readable
of all men. The German and the Irish elements,
there is reason to suspect, consort as ill together
within the one fold as ever did Guelph and Ghibel-
line of old; and it would not be the strangest thing
in all the world, if the indisposition of the faithful
laity to receive their politics from Rome were to
expand into a large unwillingness to accept foreign
dictation in any department of thought and life.
"Ultramarine" may grow to be as obnoxious an adjective in America as ever "ultramontane" was in
Europe.

With the upspringing of a genuine and general
"Old Catholic" movement among the Romanists of
the United States, many things now seemingly impossible might become possible, — among them an Eng-
lished and reformed Missal, a modified Confessional,
and a rehabilitation of the primitive Creeds as the
only œcumenical symbols of binding force. When

this state of things shall have been reached (and events in Europe as well as in America may be hastening it more rapidly than we suppose), it will be time enough to begin waving our olive branch towards the extreme right; the two religions will at least have come within speaking distance of each other.

For the present, the only hopeful outlook for non-Roman Christians seeking unity is in the direction of the great, restless, ill-compacted and ill-contented mass of reformed Christendom. To aid those who, deeply dissatisfied with things as they are, are feeling about in the dark for pillars strong enough to hold up things as they ought to be, has been the author's one endeavor.

The task set before the Christian Church in America is her familiar one of conquest; but open-eyed observers have to acknowledge that the conditions of the warfare are, in many respects, unparalleled. What we are witnessing is not the hopeful approach of a new religion to minds wholly unfamiliar with its message, but rather the painful endeavor of an old religion to maintain its hold upon a mixed multitude, already nominally under its sway, but so situated as to be peculiarly open to the temptation to revolt. The suggestion that possibly America may not continue permanently Christian is undoubtedly a painful one whether to make or to receive; but honest students of the signs of the times cannot, with a clear conscience, refuse to take it into account. To a religious

mind, that horoscope of our national destinies looks
to be infinitely the most worthy which sees in the
land that has been given us an opportunity for the
upbuilding of the Kingdom of God on earth such as
never before was put within a people's grasp. Nowhere, it would seem, so easily as here might Christian civilization, taught by the blunders of the past
and unimpeded by the rubbish of old failure, essay
to build anew the perfect city. The very fairness of
the vision is to some eyes sufficient evidence that the
dream is certain to come true. We stumble not at
believing what with the whole heart we most desire
to believe, except, indeed, when the obstacles to our
faith are of the overwhelming sort; and this ideal
picture of the new *Civitas Dei* destined to spring up
on a continent mysteriously kept out of sight until the
old errors of construction had betrayed themselves
and all things were ready for a new attempt, has
a subtile charm in it to which the imagination easily
succumbs.

But men engaged in the administration of important trusts are bound to take counsel of their just
apprehensions as well as of their sanguine hopes ;
and the Christian Church, as the trustee of the faith,
may not too confidently assume that all things will
fall out happily for her, and as they ought to do, in
this new world. Some fears are reasonable and
proper fears, and to shut our eyes on them is but
to invite them to fulfil themselves.

There are those of us who have become convinced

that only in a genuine, thorough-going, actual and visible unity is there hope for the survival of what is best in the Christian life of the Republic. But we do not desire to compass our end, or rather what we like to think of as God's purpose, by any hypocritical veiling of real difficulties, or insincere attempts to put obstacles out of existence by putting them temporarily out of mind. "Things are what they are," and no bandying of pleasant words or exchange of platform courtesies can alter the everlasting fact that unity, in order to endure, must rest on truth.

W. R. H.

New York, May 1, 1891.

CONTENTS

CONTENTS.

———•———

THE QUADRILATERAL.

I.

The Holy Scriptures of the Old and New Testaments, as "containing all things necessary to salvation," and as being the rule and ultimate standard of faith.

II.

The Apostles' Creed, as the Baptismal Symbol; and the Nicene Creed, as the sufficient statement of the Christian faith.

III.

The two Sacraments ordained by Christ Himself,— Baptism and the Supper of the Lord,— ministered with unfailing use of Christ's words of institution, and of the elements ordained by Him.

IV.

The Historic Episcopate, locally adapted in the methods of its administration to the varying needs of the nations and peoples called of God into the Unity of His Church.

I.

A PROTOCOL.

As the safety of the whole is the interest of the whole, and cannot be provided for without government, either one or more or many, let us inquire whether one good government is not, relative to the object in question, more competent than any other given number whatever. — THE FEDERALIST.

THE PEACE OF THE CHURCH

I.

A PROTOCOL.

THERE was once what was known as "the peace of the Empire." There is destined to arrive the peace of the Church. The peace of the Empire meant a civil tranquillity, brought about and held secure by a strong central force posited at Rome.

From this huge dynamo went out the threads that carried light and heat to the farthest extremities of the old Mediterranean world. It was a powerful plant that could propel energy along such tenuous conductors, and to such distances. The strength and wit of many generations had gone to the construction of the machine; but once created, it acquired a certain momentum of its own, a running force largely independent of circumstances. It was not like one of those delicate mechanisms which a grain of sand or a knot in the thread brings to a stand-still; the rollers kept their motion, and the long arms their thrust, quite regardless of petty obstructions of whatever sort. The Cæsars were merely men intrusted

with the running of the dynamo; oftener than not,
they were themselves crushed among the wheels. So
impressive was this self-perpetuating aspect of the
Empire that men came to look at the vast organism
as immortal, a thing that could not die; and secular
poets, eager to welcome back the Golden Age, could
picture to themselves no better fulfilment of their
hopes than such a stretching of the peace of the
Empire as would make it cover the whole earth. A
world

> " lapt in universal law," —

and that law Roman law, — was the goal of their
most sanguine dreams.

The Christian mind of to-day sees in all this a
divinely ordered preparation for the spread of the
gospel. The peace of the Empire made the spiritual
conquest of the Empire possible. The military roads
were as available for the evangelist as for the legion-
ary, and the imperial posts could carry epistles as
easily as rescripts.

Hence it is no wonder that when the time was
fulfilled for the so-called conversion of the Empire,
the notion should have taken possession of the minds
of many that the City of God was already come. But
really, in point of fact, the Empire never was converted. Doubtless manners were softened, jurispru-
dence modified, the general look of things a good deal
altered for the better; but the Empire, as such, ex-
perienced no change of heart. It continued what it

had always been, — a wonderfully well-contrived administrative framework, penetrated and backed by physical force. The painting of a new monogram on the plate of the machine may have served in some measure to discredit Cæsar; it implied no real enthronement of Christ.

But just because the Empire was ineligible for conversion, it became liable to fall, — and fell.

To the bulk of its immemorial possessions, — some of them precious, a good many of them embarrassing, a few deadly, — the Roman Church fell heir; and notably to the old tradition that associated efficiency with centralization. We have come, in modern times, to know more about the structure of the human body than the ancients did, and we have learned from that best of all object-lessons to anticipate in a perfect organism the distribution of centres of force.

To the Roman mind such a thought as this was wholly foreign. Unless the law went forth from Rome, how could there be unity? As this question had seemed to the emperors to admit of but one reply; so it came to seem also to the popes. Hence when the consciousness of nationality awoke strongly in the northern races, the clash followed that passes in history under the name of the Reformation.

I am not attempting a complete statement of the causes of that momentous quarrel. Besides its political character, the movement had also its still more serious doctrinal aspects. The indictment found against the Latins included the charge of a

superstitious adulteration of the ancient faith with
Pagan ingredients, as well as that of an infringement
of the ancient liberties. Were I inviting you to a
thorough analysis of the Roman Catholic controversy,
all this would have to be taken into account; but
for our immediate purpose, the effect of the Reformation upon polity is more important than its effect
upon dogma.

We are working our way towards an understanding
of the ecclesiastical state of things that confronts us
in America; and it is essential to a just appreciation
of facts as they are that we should remind ourselves
of facts as they were. There was a time then, and
that not so very long ago, when there had succeeded
to the peace of the Empire something that was supposed to be, in an equally real sense, the peace of the
Church. To be sure it was ruffled by disturbances
and heart-burnings not a few; but so, for that matter,
had the peace of the Empire been, even at its best
estate. Nevertheless, the great fact stared men in
the face that there existed a region, bounded by geographical lines more or less definite, known under the
comprehensive name of Christendom.

Throughout this tract of country certain great religious institutes found unvarying recognition and
acceptance.

One could go from land to land and find everywhere the same priesthood, the same sacraments, the
same pious usages, with which he had been familiar
in his own home from childhood. I am not now

speaking of the blemishes and drawbacks that attached to this order of things ; I am calling attention
to what was attractive, and, upon the surface at least,
admirable in it all. Certainly a traveller would not
find such privilege of sanctuary amiss to-day if he
could share it. It would add to the enjoyment of
a journey in Spain, for instance, if in a homesick
moment one could cross the threshold of Cordova's
great church, or kneel down on the floor of some
lesser house of God by the roadside, and feel that he
did so by as good a right and with as sincere a welcome as if he were native to the soil.

How can we wonder, then, that devout minds of
a conservative cast, and keenly alive to the excellen-
cies of the then existing system, should have felt
disposed to fight to the death a movement which by
implication threatened, even if it did not avowedly
assail, the integrity of this same Christendom ? And
how can we wonder that in our own days ardent and
imaginative souls, viewing the past in the warm golden
light that smooths rough outlines and makes the hard
exterior of distant objects beautiful, should have felt
disposed to insist that only by retracing their steps
and going back to the Catholic beliefs and usages of
the old days before the quarrel, could Christendom
be re-achieved?

But before we take up with that timid philosophy
of history which can see in the Reformation nothing
better than a blunder, we must consider whether any
such return to cover as the one proposed is practicable.

It is one thing to maintain an existing system against innovation, it is another and much harder task to re-establish a system that has suffered fracture. The genie of the Arabian story was with difficulty coaxed back into the casket that had been his prison. The spirit set free at the Reformation is not incapable of being housed, but it will never consent to return to quarters no roomier than those from which it broke away. Least of all can the proposal to rehabil-itate the Christendom that was before Luther and Cranmer, make a plausible showing in America. In countries that once formed a part of the Roman sys-tem, even though they lay upon the outer edge of it, a plea for reconstruction upon the old lines can boast a certain modicum of weight. When the leaders of the Anglo-Catholic movement, for example, began some fifty years ago to dream of carrying England back into "the Latin obedience," the forlornness of their hope was not at first apparent. All the forces of romanticism were on their side; they knew that they could count upon considerable dissatisfaction, born of despondency, in the liberal ranks, and there was a rallying centre ready to their hands in the old families among the nobility that through all fortunes had remained loyal to the ancient order. England had once held a place in the Roman framework; why might she not again?

Far less excuse have they who, here in America, turn for reconstructive help to Italy. Notions that were tenable in the days when the earth was supposed to be the centre of the universe, ceased to be tenable after the heliocentric astronomy had come in, and notions that were tenable under the heliocentric hypothesis as first understood, have ceased to be tenable now that we suspect that even the sun itself has motion and an orbit. No more can an ecclesiastical polity, originally fashioned to fit the Roman Empire as closely as a cloud-bank moulds itself to the landscape on which it lies, answer for the needs of a world dimensioned out of all proportion to the Christendom that used to be.

This does not necessarily mean that the Americas and Australia must needs construct for themselves forms of Church life and governance that shall stand wholly unrelated to what has gone before. That is not God's way of working, nor the way of wise men who seek to imitate the Maker's methods. The Copernican astronomy, to go back to our parable, did indeed displace, but it by no means wholly discredited the Ptolemaic astronomy. All that was true in the old system passed over into the new. The ancient observations had not lost their value because a revised grammar of their significance had come in.

There are structural principles the knowledge of which is as old as human society itself, and which no revolutions can supersede. In any future unification of the Christian body these principles will have recognition and play. They cannot be disowned, because they are written on the nature of man, and rank among the primal facts. To disentangle from whatever ought to be reckoned transitory, secondary, and adventitious, these first principles of social house-building will be my main endeavor in these lectures. It is always by returning to the true *principia*, and never by a mere going back to old times, that society, whether in its civil or its ecclesiastical form, finds safety.

It will be well to begin by considering the magnitude and complexity of the problem that offers itself for solution here in the United States, — a country which is at once the hope and the despair of believers in the reunion of Christendom; their despair, because nowhere else has the process of division and subdivision been further carried; their hope, because nowhere is there less of outward constraint to hinder a complete reconciliation, if only the true basis of amity can be found.

I invite you then to a quick review of our ecclesiastical past.

With the adoption of the Constitution, the United States became a nation, and by a stroke of the pen embarrassments innumerable that had vexed the life of the ill-compacted Confederation were put away. No such summary process of reconstruction and consolidation was possible for the scattered religious societies which from time to time during the colonial period had been planted along the Atlantic seaboard, and now found themselves, each with its own little stock of inherited prejudices and convictions, maxims of polity and formulas of faith, about starting on a new career. The time had been in the Old World when the successful assertion by a people of its proper civil unity would have been followed, as a matter of course, by the establishment of a corresponding unity ecclesiastical. The question with the England of the seventeenth century had not been whether there should or should not be an established religion, but whether the religion to be established should be Anglican, Presbyterian, or Papal. Such was not the case with the newly liberated colonies in the closing years of the century that followed the seventeenth. The day for acts of uniformity had manifestly gone by; and although to religious minds deeply impressed with the evils of sectarian strife there must have come a mingled sense of envy and self-reproach in noting the comparative ease with which the State had accomplished oneness, all sensible people settled down to the conclusion that so far as the Church was concerned the case was one in which patience must be allowed to have her perfect work. If it was a scandal, and a scandal it doubtless was, to see religion arrayed in a coat of many colors, rather than in her own proper seamless robe, there was at least the comfort of remembering that foreign weavers and old-time looms were responsible for the garment's tints and texture. It is true that the determination utterly to free religion from State control has the look of having been an after-thought with the framers of the Constitution, appearing, as it does, in the form of an amendment to that instrument, and not as one of the original articles. The fact, however, that the amendment, when proposed, excited no active opposition, and was promptly ratified, shows how wide-spread and deep-rooted in the mind of the nascent republic was the conviction that Congress ought to "make no law respecting an establishment of religion or prohibiting the free exercise thereof." That this view of the situation was shared by leading minds among the Anglican portion of the community is evidenced by the way in which the framers of the American Prayer-book expressed themselves. There were then present on our soil some ten or twelve forms of organized Christianity, of which the Anglican was one. In the face of this fact, what attitude did the Church-of-England men think it becoming in them to assume? Did they assert an ecclesiastical monopoly? Did they put forward any imperious claim to supremacy, or even to primacy? Not at all; they simply, in all humility of mind, remarked that, as a result of the political revolution that had taken place, "the different religious denominations of Christians" in what had been the Colonies, but had now become the States, had been "left at full and equal liberty to model and organize their respective churches and forms of worship and discipline in such manner as they might judge most convenient for their future prosperity, consistently with the constitution and laws of their country."[1]

This paragraph has been criticised for its naïvete, and for a lack of that proper self-assertion which

[1] See Preface to the American Book of Common Prayer.

Anglicans alive to their hereditary rights and privileges should have maintained. It was, however, the language of men who, before all else, were bent on looking the actual facts of their position in the face, undisturbed by any *a priori* theories of ecclesiastical "mission and jurisdiction."

They may have entertained individually the very strongest convictions as to the exclusive rightfulness of the Episcopal regimen ; they may have held tenaciously in their own minds to the apostolicity of liturgical worship; but they had the good judgment to perceive that to ask from their fellow-citizens anything more than a fair field and no favor would be folly. To have planted the Anglican standard in the spirit in which the last of the Bourbons hoisted at Frohsdorf the white flag of his house, crying to Orleanists, Bonapartists, and Republicans alike, " This or nothing," might have gained them the sort of admiration we accord the captain of a sinking ship who refuses to quit his quarter-deck, but it would have cost us, the children, our inheritance. White and his compeers chose a wiser course. Persuaded of the innate vitality of their principles, they cheerfully refrained from anything that might look like an arrogant assertion of them, well content to abide the working of that law of survival which, though unformulated in their day, was, in its practical bearing upon the affairs of human life, as clearly discernible then as now.

But what, in point of historical fact, were the

" different religious denominations," referred to in the preface of the Prayer-book? Roughly classified, and named in the order of their earliest organized beginnings they were these : Episcopalians (1607), Congregationalists (1620), Reformed Dutch (1628), Roman Catholics (1634), Baptists (1639), Lutherans (1669), Friends (1672), Presbyterians (1684), Mennonites (1708), Moravians (1734), Methodists (1773).[1] This list might be lengthened by expanding *genera* into *species*, — particularly in the case of the Baptists and of the Presbyterians, of which there were even then several varieties; but for the purposes of a general view the enumeration as it stands is adequate.

Ethnologically considered, the bulk of the people were of English stock ; but the Dutch, German, and Scandinavian elements were not inconsiderable, and there was also a certain small though very precious infusion of French Huguenot blood. It is evident that this is a strong Protestant showing. With the single exception of Maryland, itself largely Anglican, the newly enfranchised States may be said to have stood for the Reformation. It looked as if the two religions had divided the two Americas between them, Protestant Europe having said, I will take the North ; and Papal Europe, I will take the South. It should be acknowledged, however, that with respect to that one of the two continents with which we are the more directly interested, this remark calls for qualification. French Roman Catholics flanked the

[1] Dorchester's Christianity in the United States, pp. 35–43.

infant republic on the northeast, and Spanish Roman Catholics on the south, and both of these ante-dated, the one by nearly a century, and the other by some years, the Protestant occupancy of North America.

Such, then, was the ecclesiastical state of things at the time when this country first came forward to take her place in the family of nations. We set out upon our career pledged in the temporal order to unity, but given over in the spiritual order to what might be called, by a seeming solecism, classified confusion. In a few of the States the sanction by government of some one denomination to the discredit of the others survived the shock of the Revolution; but it was only for a little. The doctrine of establish-ments had received its death-blow; and in a few years all semblance of a desire on the part of the civil authorities to control the religious affiliations of the citizen vanished. Church and State became almost as distinctly separated as they had been before Con-stantine's day. I say "almost," because absolutely separate Church and State never can become in any country where the bulk of the people hold the Chris-tian faith. Wherever property interests and questions of contract come in, there the State has a hold. Public worship calls for a roof and walls; and where these are there is property, with all its liabilities to taxation, attachment, mortgage, confiscation and the like. The fact that a house has been consecrated to religious uses does not take it out of that area of

things material in which the State enjoys eminent
domain. Then there is marriage, a contract or a
sacrament according as we look at it from a common-
law or a canon-law standpoint. As an agreement
between two individuals, it is a matter for judges
and juries to pronounce upon; as a "holy estate"
it is the Church's affair, one of the sanctities with
which no extraneous power may intermeddle. With
limitations the same thing holds good of education
and of the administration of charity. These are
matters which the State may almost be said to have
taken up at the suggestion, or, at any rate, influenced
by the example of the Church. To put it in graphic
form, the one circle overlaps the other, and certain
interests are found resident in the space which belongs
exclusively to neither of them, while yet geometrically
a segment of each.

While, therefore, if we mean to be accurate, it is
necessary to remember that with the Christianized
peoples things secular can never be wholly severed
from things sacred, we have, speaking broadly, a
perfect right to say that the Revolution broke up
completely the old-time alliance between Church and
State, leaving the former of the two at perfect liberty
to build itself up as best it might.

Why is it then, that the Church has lagged so far
behind the State in the matter of achieving unity?
For the simple reason that the State holds and wields
the power of the sword. The thirteen colonies did
not become a republic because the people as a whole

wanted a republic, for it is notorious that many of them were at heart warmly attached to the monarchy. The republic was born of the wishes of the most part, — a most part so strong that it would have been hopeless for the lesser part to attempt resistance. The framers of the Declaration of Independence had said of governments that they derived " their just powers from the consent of the governed." By the "governed" they must of course have meant the greater number of the governed, for probably no government has ever enjoyed the unanimous good-will of those who lived under its laws. The State, in matters of the State, does not and cannot tolerate organized dissent; the law of self-preservation compels it to insist on unity. There may be, and in free countries there is entire liberty to think, and a large liberty to speak in this way or in that as to the wisdom of existing arrangements; but no attempt to act as if these arrangements did not exist is tolerated for a moment. A citizen of Pennsylvania is free to hold the opinion that the Supreme Court of that State is an unjust tribunal, and he is also free to exert himself in every way to bring about the abolition of it by legislative process; but the moment he makes bold to act in defiance of the judgments of that court he finds himself under arrest. The Bourbons stamped their cannon with the legend *Regum ratio ultima.* They were not speaking for monarchy only. All civil government, whether it be called democratic or imperial, resorts to force as its final argument. When discontent grows strong enough, and is sufficiently excited to strike back, then we have riot, rebellion, or civil war, as the case may be; but ordinarily things go on much as they would do if all men agreed. There is acquiescence even when there is not assent; so evidently true is it of a civil community, that in the ordering of its affairs it is quite impossible that every man should have his own way. That would be a singular commonwealth, indeed, which should allow the imperialists, the monarchists, the republicans, and the socialists within its borders "full and equal liberty to model and organize" their respective governments "in such manner as they might judge most convenient for their future prosperity." What keeps these various groups of theorists from attempting of their own motion so to embody their ideas, is the fact that the government actually in possession is backed by force, and will not let them do it.

But the spiritual society which we know under the name of the Church is precluded, by the very law of its being, from maintaining unity after this fashion. The Church is a "union of hearts." The power of the sword is nowhere discoverable in its charter. Its only weapon is persuasion, its only fetter the bond of charity, its only punishment a withdrawal of sacramental privilege. We have to acknowledge that often and again the Church has lost all this out of mind, and acted as if fear rather than love were the real unifying power; but in the beginning it was not so. Christ instanced the fact that his disciples were not fighting men as an evidence of the unworldly character of his kingdom. The implication was that in the building up of the new social order He had come to announce and to begin, no reliance would be placed on force. He put his followers upon their honor, and trusted them to serve Him without fear. In a common loyalty to Himself they were to find the essential motive to unity. The rest would follow in due time.

In the light of these thoughts the tardy pace at which the Church moves here in America toward the achievement of her own proper unity is easily understood. In the matter of civil organization we forced our way; in the matter of ecclesiastical organization we are feeling our way.

First of all, there has had to be awakened in men's minds a proper sense of the discredit that attaches to our present broken estate. Since denominationalism came in as a recognized state of things, all sorts of pleasant parables have been devised to make it appear lovely. Even the rainbow has been forced to lend its manifold beauty in aid of the exigencies of the argument, and we are exhorted to discern in our wretched divisions a divinely ordered variety every shade of which is essential to the full chromatic effect. Since the fathers fell asleep, all things, for the denominationalist, continue as they were from the beginning. It is his steadfast averment that matters are well enough as they are, and that it is downright ecclesiastical Quioxtism to attempt to better them.

Sometimes in defence of his view the denomination-alist presses the argument from design, sometimes the argument from despair. The Creator, he reminds us, has made men's temperaments as various as their faces. If the familiar reminder that two blades of grass are never found alike fails to convince us, we are further referred to Charles the Fifth and the story of the monastery clocks. Surely by such wealth of illustration we ought to be persuaded that the sects into which the Christian Church has let itself be splintered are really no accident, but contrari-wise the fruit of a beneficent purpose, an intelligent and harmonious design. Let us school ourselves to see in our denominations only so many flower-beds in the great garden God has planted, and in which He walks. Here are roses, there carnations, yonder lilies of the valley that love the shade; but it is all one garden, planned by one mind, laid out by one hand, fed by one sunshine.

All this has a familiar sound. We have heard it, time and again. But often when the difficulty of reconciling this pretty parable, or these pretty para-bles, with certain very distinct words of Holy Scrip-ture, not to mention certain hard facts of human life, has been pressed home so vigorously that there is no escape, the denominationalist falls back on the argu-ment from despair. True, he says, it would indeed have been most delightful could the dream of the ear-ly Fathers of the Church have been fulfilled; could Cyprian and Augustine have had their way. But it was not to be. The experiment was tried, and tried on a large scale, and it failed, and that was the end of it; there is nothing more to be said or to be attempted.

Thus what the flower-garden was to the argument from design, the shattered image becomes to the argument from despair. The experiment of unifying the Church on the plan and by the method of imperialism having come to nought, we must, forsooth, sit down with folded hands convinced that because Christendom is to-day divided, divided it must always be. And yet, so flagrant are the practical evils of denominationalism as a system; so foolish does the awkward contrivance look when we attempt to carry it to the heathen; so unsightly in real life is the result of taking it for granted that the entreaties, "Be ye all of one mind," "Mark them that cause divisions among you," "Love as brethren," were never meant to be literally understood, that even the apologists of things as they are begin to speak in broken tones, and to murmur under their breath that there must be some more excellent way if only it could be found. Not so often as of old is the voice of the orator heard on public days exulting over the number of the spires in an American village, and drawing from the spectacle his bad inference that competition in religion is as wholesome as in trade. As the battle with the common enemy waxes hot, the tactical advantage of the "moving square" becomes manifest. Economic considerations also have their weight in the mind of a people naturally thrifty, and common-sense demands to be informed why it should be necessary to keep three or four sets of parochial functionaries in pay, merely to enable three or four groups of fellow-townsmen, who differ in opinion on three or four points of belief which nobody accounts essential, to enjoy the luxury of being walled off from one another while they say their prayers.

It is no slight step taken towards unity, that this mood of dissatisfaction with the actual state of things should have become so generally prevalent. Made aware of the existence of his ailment, the sick man begins to bestir himself to find remedies ; so long as the disease lies latent there is nothing to prompt his going in search of a cure. We in America have at last reached this stage of solicitude. For a long while only a voice here and a voice there was to be heard protesting against our state of schism ; but now the complainants utter themselves in chorus. " Give peace in our time," has become common prayer.

The practical methods of attaining the desired end are reducible under three heads : —

First : The unconditional surrender of all to one.

Secondly : Confederation upon equal terms, each denomination preserving its own proper identity, but entering into formal counsel with the others with respect to all common interests.

Thirdly : Consolidation under one self-consistent and well understood system of polity and doctrine ; with ample constitutional guarantees for a permitted diversity in the methods of worship and of work.

To a study of the comparative merits of these three methods, which for the sake of convenience may be given the catch-words " Submission," " Confederation," and " Consolidation," I propose devoting the remainder of this lecture.

The foremost representative of the doctrine of unconditional surrender as the only proper pathway to unity is the Church of Rome. Let American Christians, of whatever name, forthwith give in their adhesion to the self-styled Queen and Mother of the Churches, and the thing is done, the secret of reunion has been found, the problem solved, the *Ecclesia Americana* built. There is a simplicity in the suggestion that commends it. So short a cross-path to his destination is singularly attractive to the foot-sore pilgrim, who would gladly, if he might, sing his last song of degrees, and enter with thanksgiving the city that is at unity in itself. But the maxim, " All roads lead to Rome," does not apply in lands severed from Italy by the pathless sea, and certain facts both of ancient and of contemporary history, to which we cannot shut our eyes, make dead against the notion that our help in this matter is coming to us from the seven hills.

The Roman claim, subjected to analysis, resolves itself into the following elements : (1) The *a priori* necessity of one visible head, if the Church is to exist as a corporate society on the earth. (2) The authority given to Peter to act as this visible head. (3) The transmission by Peter to his successors in

the see of Rome of the visible headship that was his.
(4) The absence of rival claimants to the supremacy.

Supplementary to these considerations, which bind
the whole world if they bind anybody, are certain
others, supposed to be specially applicable to the
United States, to wit: (5) The fact of the discovery
of the New World by a devout Roman Catholic, sail-
ing under Roman Catholic auspices. (6) The undis-
puted ecclesiastical jurisdiction exercised by the Holy
Father on this side of the ocean for more than a
hundred years before any dissentients had made their
appearance here. And finally, (7) the need of an authority backed, in a sense, by the past of all Europe,
rather than by the traditions of only a single nation,
if spiritual sovereignty is to be asserted over such a
medley of foreign stocks and races as the Republic in
this latter half of the nineteenth century has become.

It is manifestly impossible in a single lecture to
enter upon an exhaustive examination of the papal
claims; but I can and will indicate briefly the weak
points of the arguments to which I have just referred.
To urge that a visible headship is, in the very nature
of things, essential to the being of such a body as the
Church of God on earth, is in reality to beg the question at issue. When St. Paul speaks of the ascended
Christ as having been made "head over all things to
the Church," he does so without limitation or qualification. He says nothing whatever about vicar or
vicegerent. He would seem to have been haunted
by no misgiving as to the impracticability of Christ's

ruling his people from a heavenly throne. So far as centres of administration are concerned, he betrays no preference for one over another, although now and then the special personal affection for Jerusalem proper to every Hebrew heart asserts itself.

If, indeed, it could be shown that executive power is never efficiently wielded save when lodged with a dictator, then the *a priori* argument for the Papacy would have weight.

But the facts of history are against the acceptance of such a postulate. Venice under her Council and France under her Directory, to go no farther afield, are witnesses that administrative ability is not of necessity beholden solely to the "one-man power." Nothing could have been more natural than for Romans, born under the Empire, to imagine that the new society they saw emerging out of the invisible would never attain the climax of efficiency without a recognized and localized *Imperator ;* and if the theory of papal origins outlined at the beginning of this lecture be the true one, such was the way in which they did actually reason. But to us looking at the matter in the light of the Empire's decline and fall, as well as of its birth and growth, it is by no means axiomatic that human society to be well ordered must needs discover and acknowledge in some one mortal man its visible controller. The universe as a whole, so Christians believe, is governed by council. We recognize in Deity something other and better than the bare expression of singleness. Why then assume that of necessity the oversight of the Holy Catholic Church in order to be thorough must be lodged with a solitary potentate ? The world secular is to-day kept in tranquillity by forces emanating from London, Paris, Berlin, St. Petersburg, and Washington, as completely as it ever was when all power centred at Rome. If such can be the case in the temporal order, why not also in the spiritual ?

But what if our Lord, it is asked, did actually give to Simon Peter the prerogative of supremacy ? Why then, of course, for Christians the case is closed, and *a priori* reasons either for or against become at once irrelevant. We pass therefore from abstract to historical ground, and look to see what the New Testament has to say, or may be supposed to say, in support of the Roman claim. It would seem on general principles as if the Epistles credited to St. Peter himself ought to yield the desired evidence. The encyclical letters of the pontiffs who are supposed to hold from him have never been reticent with respect to prerogative ; and if St. Peter was conscious of possessing rights of supremacy over the whole Church, nothing could have been more natural than that the fact should leave its impress on his correspondence. And yet we look in vain to this quarter for a single sentence corroborative of the claims of the Popes. The Apostle does indeed exhort the elders of the Church, but he is careful to do it as one who is " also an elder." In fact, had he been expressly aiming to avoid the assertion of an authority different from and superior to

that of his fellow Apostles, he could scarcely have
chosen a tone better fitted for his purpose than that
which pervades the whole range of his writings. A
similar poverty of allusion, or rather entire absence of
allusion, to the Petrine claim is observable in the
other Epistles; and when it comes to the Book of
Acts, Paul is so clearly the hero of the story that
Peter's prominence in the earlier chapters is almost
lost out of mind before we reach the end. When the
case has been narrowed down, as it must be, to the
four Gospels, we discover that the real issue hangs
on the right interpretation of three palmary passages;
that which records Peter's confession of Jesus as the
Christ, and our Lord's answering declaration;[1] that
in which Christ assures Peter of His having prayed
for him that his faith fail not;[2] and that in which,
after the resurrection, Christ with a most noticeable
earnestness exhorts Peter by the love he bears Him,
"Feed my sheep."[3]

Upon these three texts the Scriptural argument for
the Papacy really rests. What shall we say to them?
Briefly this, that so far as the earliest commentators
on the New Testament are concerned, the Fathers of
the primitive Church, the weight of testimony is
wholly against the papal interpretation. It was only
after the Holy See had established itself by other
means that there was read into these passages the

---

[1] St. Matt. xvi. 13–20; St. Mark viii. 27–29; St. Luke ix.
18–20.

[2] St. Luke xxii. 31, 32.   [3] St. John xxi. 15–18.

sense which Roman controversialists now allege as
the only proper one. In the case of the first of the
three passages some of the Fathers see in Christ's
words " this rock " an allusion to Himself, that one
foundation other than which no man can lay ; some
understand it to signify the truth of our Lord's divinity to which Peter had just borne the earliest human
witness ; while still others connect the promise with
those providential features in Peter's personal history
which made him the first stone in that great edifice,
the building of which is still in progress. In a true
sense the Church began with Peter, for it was he who
led at Pentecost, and it was he whose first use of " the
keys of the kingdom of heaven " threw open to the
nations the door that had been shut against them so
long. But Jerusalem and Cæsarea, not Rome, are
the geographical names we associate with these
greatest of the acts of Peter ; and there lies a wide
gap between assent to the primacy of this foremost
of the Twelve, and consent to the doctrine that
dominion has been given to the Bishops of Rome even
to the end of the world.

The fact of Peter's leadership among the disciples,
in itself sufficiently evidenced by the position given
to his name in all of the lists, is a sufficient clew to
the meaning of the second of the great papal texts.
Nothing could be more natural than the singling
out for special prayer the man who had been bold to
say, " Thou art the Christ, the son of the living God,"
and nothing could have been more natural than to

select him to be the strengthener of his brethren in their hour of need; but that this strengthening function was not peculiar to the Apostle Peter is evident from its being associated in the New Testament with no fewer than four of St. Peter's colleagues in the work of evangelization.

With respect to the scene upon the shore of the sea of Tiberias, where Jesus said to Simon Peter once, "Feed my lambs," twice, "Feed my sheep," the last of the alleged Gospel evidences in behalf of the Papacy, it would seem to be enough simply to put in contrast the view which sees in it an exclusive bestowal of ecclesiastical jurisdiction, and that which discerns, rather, a singularly tender and touching suggestion of a duty that appertains to every shepherd of souls as such. Peter had three times denied his Master; three times, therefore, does the Master reestablish Peter in his pastoral office; but His doing so in no sense disestablishes the rest. If any mystical and symbolic inference with respect to the perpetual government of the Church is to be forced out of this beautiful closing chapter of the Fourth Gospel, it would seem as if St. John, rather than St. Peter, ought to have the benefit of it, for of him are those strange words written, "If I will that he tarry till I come, what is that to thee?" If this thing had been said of Simon Peter, what volumes of rhetoric might it not have furnished to the upholders of the papal claim?

But the Roman Catholic argument from the New Testament is supplemented by another from tradition.

St. Peter, we are assured, was the first bishop of Rome, and as such transmitted his plenary powers to those who have succeeded him in that see, from Linus, the first, to Leo XIII., the latest of them.

Protestant writers who spend their strength in trying to prove that St. Peter never was at Rome make a mistake. Very possibly they are right; but it is proverbially hard to prove a negative, and in making so much effort to demonstrate this particular negative they betray a misgiving that unless it can be done the case is lost. Even when it has been conceded that St. Peter, in the course of his travels, may have visited Rome, it by no means follows that he was either the exclusive founder or the first bishop of the Roman Church. St. Paul prided himself on never trespassing on the missionary fields of other Apostles. But we have among St. Paul's writings a letter to the Church of the Romans. Would he have been likely to write his Epistle had there been a bishop in charge at Rome? And supposing that bishop to have been no less a dignitary than the Apostle Peter, should we find no reference made to him in the long list of salutations with which the writer closes his communication?

An early author of repute (Irenæus) makes St. Peter and St. Paul jointly the founders of the Roman Church. According to him, Linus was the first bishop of the series, not the second, and received his commission at the hands of both of the great Apostles. A happy omen this of the better day to come, when St. Peter, as the representative of ecclesiastical order, and St. Paul, as the representative of the freedom that comes with faith, shall strike hands in that "Holy Catholic Church" in which, spite of all set-backs and discouragements, those who say the Apostles' Creed continue to believe.[1]

But it is still further urged that, in the absence of any other claimant, Rome ought to hold supremacy by virtue of her being, so to speak, the residuary legatee. If Jerusalem, or Antioch, or even Alexandria had maintained an unbroken line of bishops from the beginning, there might be grounds for partitioning the sovereignty among all the survivors, but inasmuch as Rome is actually the only survivor, ought not the whole inheritance to be hers?[2]

Yes, perhaps so, if we can agree about what the inheritance is. If it be simply an inheritance of fair fame, certainly all who value what is ancient for its own sake, and who hold that what is time-honored ought to be by man honored as well, will concede the thing asked for not only cheerfully but thankfully. There never has been a time when the Church of Rome, if content to be the Church of Rome, would not have received from the rest of Christendom her

[1] For an admirable summary of the heads of the Roman controversy, see Dr. Salmon's "Infallibility of the Church," a work characterized by the late Von Döllinger as one of the great polemical achievements of the century.

[2] See "A Letter to his Grace the Duke of Norfolk, on occasion of Mr. Gladstone's recent Expostulation," by John Henry Newman, D.D., of the Oratory, London, 1875, p 26, § 3.

full measure of respect. It is not against the Church of Rome, it is against the self-styled Mother and Mistress of all the Churches that we have made war, or rather are defending ourselves.

But just as the disproof of the Scriptural argument for the supremacy of St. Peter turned the flank of the argument from tradition, so the disproof of the *a priori* argument for the necessity of a single visible headship over the Church, may be said to have anticipated the defeat of this argument from survival. If it could be proved that the Church absolutely required for its efficiency the recognition of a supreme Pontiff, why then the fact that there lived within our horizon only one pretender to the post would unquestionably make the claim of such survivor a very strong one. But if, on the other hand, the supposition in question be, as we have seen that it is, a wholly gratuitous one, why then Rome's cry, "Come unto me, for there is none other whom it is possible for you to seek," falls dead.

There remain to be considered the supplementary arguments that are supposed to make Rome's contention a particularly strong one in the case of the United States.

It is hardly possible to take seriously the argument that because Christopher Columbus was a Roman Catholic, therefore all of us who occupy the new world he discovered ought to be of his religion. In the fifteenth century all Europe was under the Papacy; the note of revolt had not yet been sounded, and if America was to be discovered by a European it must needs be a Roman Catholic who should discover it. The planting of the cross on the soil of San Salvador was indeed an act of high significance; but the Papacy can scarcely claim an exclusive interest in the cross, a symbol that had acquired its significance long before St. Peter is alleged even to have seen Rome.

The claim founded upon a long continued assertion of ecclesiastical jurisdiction in the New World, would carry greater weight in this connection than it does, if it could be shown that the jurisdiction was ever to any considerable extent either exercised or acknowledged on the Atlantic seaboard in the colonial period; or in other words, had the people who in 1789 constituted themselves a republic, ever recognized the right of the Roman Pontiff to reign over them. We know that the contrary was notoriously the fact. Perhaps a moiety of the Marylanders were Roman Catholic; but over against these stood multitudes whose very presence here was owing to their hatred of whatever even so much as approximated to the religion of Rome. In the Spanish possessions, and in what had been the French, the Roman Catholic Church had an unquestioned foothold; but Canada and Florida lay beyond the limits of the Republic, and what was true of them was not true of it. Substantially this was an Englishman's country when it set out upon its course, and it was England that had been " the bulwark of the Reformation."

Yes, the Roman Catholic replies, an Englishman's country it was once, but an Englishman's country it long ago ceased to be. Europe has poured itself into America, and to-day what is needed to effect the unifying process is such a power as can appeal to memories that are common to all the nationalities of the Old World. There is no such power, save the Papacy.

The answer to this is two-fold. A reconciliation imposed upon us from abroad and by an extraneous power is not the sort of reconciliation of which we are in search. As a people, we think that we can best settle our family quarrel among ourselves. But aside from this, is there not good reason to think that the extent of the Europeanizing process covered by the last fifty years has been grossly exaggerated? It is true that there has been an immense infusion of foreign blood; but is it true that this has sufficed really to overmaster the original strain? There is good authority for the statement that of the people now inhabiting the territory of the United States considerably more than half are the direct descendants of grandparents or great-grandparents who were living here in the year 1800. Moreover, law and language are forces that link us almost indissolubly to an English past. Our common law is English. The "free institutions" of which we are so proud are of English parentage. Above all, our speech is English. The affectionate appeals of the Holy Father calling us back to our allegiance have to be translated. The ring of the sentences is sonorous, but our ears miss the mother element. The children of our public schools, from whatever quarter of the globe they may have come, are taught to think, to speak, to write in English. Sentences from the great masters of English letters, snatches of English oratory, couplets of English verse creep into their minds, and stay there moulding thought and action in a thousand unsuspected ways. The importance of this fact it is quite impossible to overstate. Here and there in the vast stretch of our possessions little areas are to be found where bi-lingual education has to be tolerated for a time; but it is only for a time. The English language has a grasp upon this country that can by no means be shaken off, and even race distinctions, deeply rooted as they are, must sooner or later inevitably yield to the formative touch of this all-conquering tongue. As yet, the Roman ecclesiastics and theologians, born Roman, have not acquired the power of writing English with much force. In this department of their propaganda they have been dependent on recruits from the Anglican ranks. Until they shall have acquired this gift of utterance, the mere fact that the population of the United States, classified by its race affinities, represents the whole of Europe, will not greatly help their missionary effort.

I have thought it right to deal thus promptly with the Roman Catholic claims, for the simple reason that if these are valid, any further discussion of means and methods must prove superfluous. If our first duty as Christians be to obey the voice that says to us from Peter's chair, " Come unto me," why then

the case is closed.   America, on that supposition, has
only to do what England did when Queen Mary succeeded to King Edward, namely, to haul down the
flag of the Reformation, and to give up the ship.

There is, however, an alternative form of unconditional surrender to which I ought perhaps to make
at least a passing reference before we take our final
leave of this first of the three theories of unity, the
theory of submission. There are a few souls sanguine enough to imagine it possible that the absolute
submission refused to the Roman Pontiff, may still
be secured at the dictate of the Anglican Episcopacy.
Let all dissentients at once give in their allegiance
to the Protestant Episcopal Church ; conform to the
canons of the General Convention, and consent to
worship publicly no otherwise than in accordance
with the rubrics of the Book of Common Prayer, and
the thing is done.   We have our Church of America
off-hand and without vexatious delay.   But if Angli-
canism pure and simple, with all the adventitious aids
it enjoys in the land of its birth, with all the charm
that ancient architecture can lend and all the prestige old national traditions and long inherited titles
avail to foster, has nevertheless failed to keep within
one fold even the half of the people of Great Britain,
is it to be supposed that any new summons, issued at
this late day, " Go to, become forthwith what we
are," is likely to win submission.

Happily it has ceased to be any longer necessary to
argue seriously against this form of the doctrine of un-

conditional surrender, for the reason that the bishops of the English-speaking race, in council assembled, have themselves given it a quietus. By the Declaration set forth at Chicago in 1886, and ratified at Lambeth in 1888, the Anglican Communion throughout the world committed itself, so far as by the voice of its chief pastors it could be committed, to a far larger and more generous platform of unity than any of which the framers of the Act of Uniformity ever dreamed. But I am anticipating matters by this reference. I was led into making it because otherwise our study of the various phases of the submission doctrine would have been incomplete.

We have next to consider the theory of ecclesiastical unity through confederation, the second of the three methods that have found advocates. The confederative theory contemplates some such combination of the various religious bodies of the land as would exist in the case of labor unions, were there a single General Assembly empowered to legislate for them all in matters of common interest, while yet each separate union retained control over the affairs of its own trade. Under this scheme denomination-alism would not cease to be, but its more flagrant evils might conceivably be diminished; the conduct of missions, for example, being relegated to the General Assembly, and the heathen thus saved the scandal of being called to look upon a piebald Christianity. In short " confederation " is but another name for some

modus vivendi under which we might live along together very much as we are living now, only in rather
pleasanter mutual relations than at present, with more
of concert and with less of friction. That the proposal has a certain plausibility upon the face of it,
it is needless to deny. It has the great advantage of
involving a minimum of change. So deep rooted have
our denominational traditions grown to be, so vast are
the property interests at stake, so complicated is the
network of missionary and educational enterprise to
which the various religious bodies stand committed,
that any scheme of unity which proposes at the outset
to hold all these things harmless and to ensure their
integrity for an indefinite time future, is sure to win
at least a momentary approval.

But confederation weighed in the balances is found
wanting. In itself considered, it is the weakest of all
the forms of unity, and the least stable. Its proper
symbol is the fagot, which has unity indeed, but
unity of a very precarious sort, fragile, ill-compacted,
easily terminable. The parts of a confederacy are
mechanically not chemically combined ; they hold
together less by affinity than by cohesion. Confederacy has no power to weather tribulation, the mere
touch of trouble makes shipwreck of it. We Americans tried confederation as our first experiment in
the direction of national unity ; and a very poor thing
we found it. Our Constitution grew directly out of
a desire for " a more perfect union " than the mere
bundling process of confederation could bring to pass.

In fact, there are no two words in the political vocabulary of Americans more conspicuously ill-omened than "confederacy" and "confederation." They are words synonymous with transitoriness and failure; no slightest promise of permanence is to be found in them. If all this be true of the confederative idea as it stands related to national interests and the life of states, how much more impracticable is the application of the principle to our ecclesiastical condition. If the confederation of communities each of which occupies a well-ascertained geographical area, and has a certain personal identity of its own, is a thing compassed about with difficulty, what shall we say to a scheme that proposes to bind together by treaty ties social organizations that already cover the same space, and recognize no territorial boundary lines?

We can imagine France resolving itself into a confederacy, and giving to each one of its present Departments a sovereignty of its own. Such an act would be a step backward, but it is conceivable. Is it conceivable, however, that the French, in despair over their partisan condition, should vote to allow the adherents of each of the great parties to organize according to its own notion of political wisdom, — the Bonapartists carrying on an empire, the Legitimists an absolute monarchy, the Orleanists a limited monarchy, the Moderates a republic, and the Reds a commune, all at the same time, and within the limits of the same France, — provided only they agree to fashion themselves into a confederation? This is really, when we look the facts in the face, what Christian Unity would mean here in America under a scheme of denominational confederation. It would be an attempt to knit together for working purposes methods of polity that from the very nature of things cannot co-exist in one and the same system. It would be a clearing-house, not a Church.

Denominational confederation has been ably urged upon us under the attractive phrase, " The United Churches of the United States." [1] If one might be permitted to drop out two letters from this taking title, so that it should read " The United Church of the United States," the words would then express the very thing we need. But the lurking fallacy in the expression as it stands is this ; a parallelism is suggested which does not exist. The " States " that make up the national Union are territorial and social entities, each of which has its well-defined metes and bounds ; whereas the Churches out of which it is proposed to construct the ecclesiastical Union are bodies of men scattered, with a greater or less evenness of distribution, over the whole country, and, what is still more to the point, each of them organized with

---

[1] See " The United Churches of the United States," by the Rev. Charles W. Shields, D. D., in the " Century Magazine " for November, 1885. The allusion in the text must by no means be understood as indicating any failure on the writer's part to appreciate the immense value of the service rendered by Professor Shields to the cause of Christian unity. No one has done more than he to waken in the people of this country a sense of wholesome shame at the spectacle of their " unhappy divisions."

a view to ministering to the spiritual needs of the whole country. If the supposed case of the confederated labor-unions be urged as furnishing a more serviceable analogy, the reply is obvious, that the various trades although not segregated in space are segregated as respects the ends they have severally in view. They have therefore a certain separateness that makes confederation possible. The Bricklayers' Union aspires to do all the bricklaying, and the Carpenters' Union aspires to do all the joinery-work needed by the people of the United States. The bricklayers have no desire to touch a single stick of timber, nor do the carpenters wish to lay a single brick. Not such is the case as it stands between the Baptists and the Presbyterians. The Baptists have it for their aim, so far as in them lies, to make Christians of all the people of the land ; and the Presbyterians have it for their aim to do the very same thing. Unless they can find a better sort of unity than " confederation " offers, they must from the very nature of the case continue what they are now, rivals in the same field, competitive rather than co-operant.

With " submission " and " confederation," both of them discarded, there remains as a final resort the method of consolidation ; more fully defined already as a union under one self-consistent and well-understood system of polity and doctrine, with ample constitutional guarantees for a permitted diversity in the methods of worship and of work. The theory of consolidation differs from the theory of submission which it may be charged with resembling in this, that although it does undoubtedly presuppose the selection of one denomination from among the rest to form a rallying centre, it provides at the same time for the generous inclusion and careful conservation of whatever the re-entering companies of believers count most precious among their heirlooms. Every one of the great denominations has its own hallowed memories, its own roll of martyrs, its own cherished manner of worship, its own long-tried methods of missionary work, above all its own revered type of Christian character. There is no reason why sudden violence should be done to these sacred things. The theory of submission would compel their prompt abandonment. The theory of consolidation supposes not only their permitted but their constitutionally guarded continuance. Take divine service, for example; consolidation would not involve the displacement of extemporaneous methods of worship among those who value them, by an insistence upon either the Missal or the Prayer-book, but on the contrary would guard the preferences of the non-liturgical families in the one household as jealously as it would protect those whose traditions were of the other sort. There would be nothing to forbid the recognition, in a truly Catholic American Church, of a Puritan rite, an Anglican rite, a Latin rite, and a German rite. Such diversities of method in the line of worship might perfectly well co-exist under one general and comprehensive scheme of polity. Such titles as " Episcopalian," and " Presbyterian," and "Congregationalist" would have to go by the board, because these would indicate a real schism in the body, a state of things like that just now supposed in the case of a re-organized France; but the disappearance of these names would by no means necessarily involve the loss of anything that is really precious in the spiritual possessions of the communions at present burdened with them. In fact it would be a distinct impoverishment, rather than a gain, were we to lose the fine types of character which the denominations I have mentioned have severally cultivated and matured. We should be merging our differences to little purpose, if in the process we were to forfeit any considerable portion of the treasures accumulated by the several tribes during their years of exile and separation. In the Catholic Church of America there must be room for the stern virtues of the Covenanter, as well as for the gentler qualities that make the devout follower of George Fox lovable, and the Anglican type of sainthood attractive. True catholicity can never come about as the result of either an eclectic or a levelling process. There is nothing manufactured or artificial about it. It never was or will be made to order. It manifests itself spontaneously and grows as the flowers grow, when once the multitude of the brethren consent to dwell together in unity. How, then, can even so much as a beginning be made? Supposing what I have called consolidation upon a definite and well-understood basis, or, as it might be otherwise expressed, crystallization about a fixed nucleus, to have been accepted as the true principle; by what law of natural or spiritual selection can we imagine the desired discrimination wrought, the right basis or nucleus determined? We can think of various possible criteria, by aid of which a decision might be reached, if only all could be counted upon to acquiesce in, and to abide by the result. There is, for example, the criterion of antiquity. Were this test accepted (as, taken by itself, it certainly would not be), the question would be narrowed down to a choice between the Episcopal and the Roman Catholic Churches, both of which bodies have an historic life that antedates the Reformation. Again, there is the criterion of numbers, — a favorite standard of judgment with all democracies. Were this accepted, the Methodists or the Baptists would have claims such as no competing organizations could dispute. Yet again, Congregationalists and Presbyterians might very properly plead the large influence their ideas have exercised upon the growth of American institutions, as a reason why one or other of them should be taken as the basis of the United Church. Between them these two bodies dominated the period of the English Commonwealth, and if the Republic be, as in a real sense and in a certain measure it undoubtedly is, the child of the Commonwealth and the heir of its political philosophy, that in itself is a strong *prima facie* argument in favor of entrusting our ecclesiastical destinies to the same hands that under God have so largely shaped our national and civil fortunes.

But even supposing ourselves to have reached a point where we acknowledge that a choice between these various rallying centres is desirable, there still remains the stubborn question, Who is to choose? There is no dictator who can settle the point by throwing his sword into the scale; for we have agreed that this is a matter to which the sword is wholly irrelevant, and we have ruled dictators out of court. Resort to the ballot would be ludicrous, and a general election impossible. The putting of the Roman Empire up at auction was a scandal, but the sending of all Christians to the polls to vote upon a proposed constitution for the Kingdom of Heaven would be a greater.

No, there is nothing to be done, but for each of the existing organizations of those within our borders who profess and call themselves Christians, to apply itself to the study of the problem, and having done so to set forth in the fewest and plainest words possible, the result of its thinking. Let us hear from each denomination what, in its deliberate judgment, is the most generous platform of union it can conscientiously offer to the rest. Once in possession of these *ultimata* our American Christendom as a whole will be in a far better condition to form a judgment than it is to-day. When it is found, as doubtless it will be found, that the resemblances between the various formulas of concord are far more striking than the differences, such a cry for unity will go up from the whole nation as shall assuredly enter into the ears of the Lord of Sabaoth and bring the answer He alone can give.

One of our denominations, as it happens, has done this very thing already, and is first in the field with its suggestion of the true basis of unity. The suggestion may be a mistaken one. There may inhere in it some fatal logical or historical flaw. It claims no note of infallibility, but as a suggestion it has at least one merit, the merit of having been made.

The Chicago-Lambeth platform, as it may fairly enough be called, sets forth that the data essential to the establishment of a visible unity among Christians are as follows : —

First. The Holy Scriptures of the Old and New Testament as containing all things necessary to Salvation, and as being the rule and ultimate standard of faith.

Secondly. The Apostles' Creed as the Baptismal symbol ; and the Nicene Creed, as the sufficient statement of the Christian Faith.

Thirdly. The two Sacraments ordained by Christ Himself, — Baptism and the Supper of the Lord, — ministered with unfailing use of Christ's words of institution, and of the elements ordained by Him.

Fourthly. The Historic Episcopate, locally adapted in the methods of its administration to the varying needs of the nations and peoples called of God into the unity of his Church.[1]

This is the answer of the Bishops of the Anglican

[1] Official Report of the Lambeth Conference of 1888, p. 86.

faith and order throughout the world to the question, What do Anglicans account the minimum of agreement prerequisite to any practical steps toward the achievement of a *bona fide* unity? My purpose in these lectures will be to unfold the contents of this utterance of theirs, and to set forth as clearly as possible the bearings of it. Firmly persuaded myself of the solidity of the ground taken by the Bishops, I do not pretend to an attitude of indifferentism, but frankly confess myself an advocate. It is needless to say that I speak with no authority other than that of one who has given the subject patient thought. In the last resort the Bishops must be their own interpreters; no commentator can force a meaning upon their words which they themselves are unwilling to avow. And yet it is to be remembered that the general judgment of mankind is but the aggregate of the personal judgments of the members of the race; and however valueless a solitary expression of opinion or belief may seem, those who sit over against the treasury of truth do ill to flout it altogether.

The coral insect lives and dies far down under the surface of the sea. A tiny speck of solid substance hidden out of sight is all his memorial. By and by, overhead there rises up an island; groves of palm are on it; birds build their nests there, and at last men their homes.

II.

THE ARCHIVES.

The Christian character in its completeness is the result and outgrowth of all that series of events of which the Bible is in part, but in the most important part, the record . . . The Bible exhibits it in various stages, in various forms, not always perfect, yet always going on to what is higher and purer, and shown to us at last, after the passage of so many ages and generations, so many efforts and failures and slow steps of progress, in its finished and flawless perfectness in the person of the divine Son of Man. — RICHARD WILLIAM CHURCH.

I have been forced by the peculiar circumstances of my work to regard from many sides the difficulties which beset our historic faith. If I know by experience their significance and their gravity; if I readily allow that on many points I wish for fuller light; then I claim to be heard when I say without reserve that I have found each region of anxious trial fruitful in blessing; that I found my devout reverence for every word of the Bible quickened and deepened, when I have acknowledged that it demands the exercise of every faculty with which I have been endowed, and, that as it touches the life of man at every point, it welcomes for its fuller understanding the help which comes from every gain of human knowledge. — BROOKE FOSS WESTCOTT.

I have always been strongly in favor of secular education, in the sense of education without theology; but I must confess I have been no less seriously perplexed to know by what practical measures the religious feeling, which is the essential basis of conduct, was to be kept up, in the present utterly chaotic state of opinion upon these matters, without the use of the Bible. — THOMAS HENRY HUXLEY.

II.

THE ARCHIVES.

First in their list of essentials the Bishops at Lambeth placed the Hebrew and Christian Scriptures, characterizing them thus : " *The Holy Scriptures of the Old and New Testaments, as ' containing all things necessary to salvation,' and as being the rule and ultimate standard of faith.*"

The statement that Holy Scripture " containeth all things necessary to salvation " has a positive and a negative side. Positively, it asserts that in Holy Scripture " things necessary to salvation " are to be found ; negatively, it withholds from any and every extra-Scriptural demand upon our faith, the power to bind. The statement, on its affirmative side, does not allege that a knowledge of all things in Holy Scripture is necessary to salvation ; nor yet on its negative side does it declare that nothing beyond the range of Holy Scripture is good to be believed ; but that which by implication is averred is, that if we want to find the things essential to the soul's safety, we shall do well to look into the Scriptures rather than elsewhere to find them ; and that which by implication is denied is, that anything over and above what Scripture sets forth ought to be counted among the possessions which the soul must have if it would escape eternal loss. On the one hand, therefore, the statement is exclusive of the merely literary view which sees in the Bible only one among many collections of writings alleged to be sacred; while, on the other, it opposes itself to the Roman Catholic doctrine that we must supplement Scripture by Tradition if we wish to be well assured of " all things necessary to salvation." Accordingly, I propose to take up in this connection the general question, — How ought we of these times to think about the Bible? Or, to put it otherwise, Has anything occurred in the intellectual movement of our day to compel a change of attitude on the part of reasonable men towards the book, or books, heretofore dignified by the title Word of God? Have such words as " revelation " and " inspiration " really become meaningless, or if not quite meaningless, at any rate so thoroughly diluted as to be void of any distinctive flavor? In short, do the Bishops betray themselves as men belated and behind their time when they speak to us of the Bible as being " the rule and ultimate standard of faith " ? I make bold to answer these questions in the negative. I hope to be able to give sound reasons for believing that the unique character hitherto conceded to the Christian Scriptures is destined to continue to attach to them; that the Bible substantially as it is may be counted upon to survive the shock of criticism, and to stand, as it has stood, the accredited classic of religion, a hand-book of belief indispensable to man.

My method will not be that of minute inquiry into questions of date and authorship connected with the various books of the Bible, a task for which I am not adequately furnished, and which I could only accomplish as a borrower; but, instead, such a discussion of the first principles involved in the question at issue, as will demand of those whom I address no other preparative than that always praiseworthy possession, an open mind. I cannot help thinking that on such a line I shall better succeed in justifying the prominence given in the Lambeth platform to the Holy Scriptures of the Old and New Testaments, than if I were to bewilder you with citations and overload your memories with dates.

Can God disclose his mind to man?

Has He at any time or times actually done so?

Is there record of such disclosure or disclosures?

Have we such a record in the writings that collectively make up the Bible?

These are simple questions which it is perfectly possible to deal with in a plain and intelligible way. To have them answered for us is to have the mind set permanently at rest with respect to what is most central to religion.

I begin with the remark that so far as the intellectual life of the race is concerned, there can be no denying that it has, from time to time, received impulse and acceleration from the impact of new truth announced at the lips of men called discoverers. Sometimes in groups and clusters, sometimes singly

and at long intervals, men have come upon the scene
equipped to teach their fellow-men things not before
known. The gap that separates these men of genius,
as they are commonly called, from the rank and file
of their fellow-students in the lower class-room is
so portentously wide, that evolution is overtaxed in
the effort to account for their appearance upon any
theory of progress by infinitesimal increments. It is
true that we must distinguish between such discoveries as are the product of profound and long-sus-
tained reflection, and those that have been happened
upon by what we call chance. In the case of certain
discoveries, that of anæsthesia, for example, there is
no evidence of genius whatsoever. The thing was
blundered into, not reasoned out; and the same may
be said of countless chance findings that pass in the
books under the same general head with those great
disclosures that have followed upon hard thinking.
The mere discovery of a new star, or of a hundred
new stars, is a small matter as compared with the
glory of discerning, for the first time, one of the
structural principles involved in the celestial me-
chanics; and even to have added an item to the cat-
alogue of the chemical elements is an achievement
in no measure comparable with the working out of
a fresh rationale of the molecular motions. Of the
discoverers of great principles my remark holds good,
that the difference between them and other men is
so sharply accentuated as almost to warrant us in
thinking it one of kind rather than of degree.

Of such men as Galileo and Newton, the most natural account would seem to be that they were sent into the world so marvellously endowed for the express purpose of communicating a message and bestowing a blessing. If the universe had a conscious designer, and all theists, whether Christian or not, must so believe, the great truths of the mathematics are common to his mind and to ours. That one after another of these truths should have come to light among us, we are accustomed to explain by saying that Euclid lived, that Kepler lived; but why not go farther back, and say: God lives, who by the lips of his servant Euclid has taught us the properties of angles, and at the mouth of his servant Kepler has revealed to us the principles of curves? Of course it is possible for the materialist to block any such movement back towards the purposeful Author and Maker by a flat denial of any consciousness in the universe other than that of which each one of us knows himself to be possessed; but, as I just intimated, my appeal is to the theists, not to the atheists. Under a theistic scheme of evolution, nothing could be more reasonable than to picture God educating his creature man by a succession of messengers empowered to impart truth as fast as the pupil shall be found "able to bear it." Not only so; we can imagine Him using races as well as individuals for teachers, and as apprenticing man first to this people, then to that, according to the need to be met. Such a theory has, of course, its margin of unexplained phenomena; it does not satisfactorily account for everything; but is there a single one among the great generalizations of science that can show a map with no shadowed patches, no tracts or even zones that have to be marked "unexplored"? Accepted as a working hypothesis, the theistic interpretation of history clears up a greater number of dark places than any other interpretation that has been suggested. As a matter of fact, we find the world indebted for its advancement to certain definite individuals, and to certain definite races, as to no other individuals and to no other races. The whole family has been in pupilage to one great man after another; to one select race after another; has gone to school, as we may say, now in Phœnicia, now at Athens, now at Jerusalem. To discover a purpose in all this, to catch the outline of a plan, is surely not the unintelligent thing some would have us account it. If there be a more reasonable method of explaining what our eyes see, let us by all means be told what it is.

The link between these thoughts and the subject in hand is obvious. The Christian plea for the Scriptures is that they contain disclosures not elsewhere to be found with respect to the character and purposes of God, and the duty and destiny of man. It is not asserted that no intimations upon these weighty matters are to be found in literatures other than the Hebrew, for one need only be tolerably well-informed in order to know that the contrary is the fact. But intimations are very different things from disclosures.

The Christian contention is that to one selected people, there was given for the sake of, and with a view to, all the other peoples of the earth, a knowledge of certain great verities wholly undiscoverable by the ordinary processes of human intelligence. It is one thing for a document to be generally pervaded by what we may call a religious or spiritual tone; the sacred books of the East give voluminous evidence that such is the case. But it is quite another thing for a writing to acquire sacredness because of the serious and downright way in which it sets forth such statements as that God has sent his Son into the world, that Christ is risen from the dead, that the time is coming in which there shall be new heavens and a new earth. These, and the like, are announcements as distinct, and certainly as grave, as the announcement, " The world goes around the sun;" " Every particle of matter attracts every other particle with a force inversely proportional to the square of the distance." Moreover, it is to be observed that the truths in question are not presented to us in the Bible as the outcome of the broodings of devout souls; they are put into the form of messages. God, it is declared, has sent us word that things are thus and so between Him and us, and that certain events are destined to come to pass for which we are bound to be ready.

I lay stress upon this point in the hope that by doing so I may disabuse some minds of the notion that if we will only be patient, natural science, which has already done so much to widen the area of our knowledge,

will confer upon us the still further boon of a demonstrable religion. Natural science deals with number,
mass, and force ; it can count and weigh and register ;
but of the relations of persons to one another it
neither knows nor professes to know anything at all.
No conceivable enlargement of our acquaintance with
the material world can ever give us the answer to the
weightier questions of religion, for these are all of
them personal. Even though the arithmetic of the
heavens and the earth were to be worked out to the last
figure, — every star tabulated, every period computed,
every atom weighed, — we should still be as far as ever
from finding the solution of the problems that lie
most heavily upon the mind. If God have what we
understand by personality, that is to say, self-con-
sciousness and will, we as persons must stand related
to Him in some definite way ; He must have a purpose
with respect to us, and we a duty towards Him.

But how can natural science help us here ? It can
indeed throw some light upon the care that must be
taken of the body, if it is to be kept healthy ; and
since man's trusteeship of his five senses is a doctrine of religion, we need not deny to such sciences
as anatomy and physiology, a certain auxiliary value
in making us more fully acquainted with our duty
towards God. But the care of the body is only one
department of religion. Man is not adequately considered when we think of him only in his solitariness
as an individual. Account has to be taken of the
thousand and one complications that arise as soon as

you bring man into contact with his fellow-men, and look at him in the light of father, brother, neighbor, townsman, citizen.

In this region of man's social relations, natural science, strictly so called, can help us not at all. Such mixed sciences as sociology and political economy can indeed throw light upon the matter; they can minister to the needs of the body politic, just as we have seen that anatomy and physiology can minister to the needs of the body physical; but even they, when confronted with the blunt question, Why must I do right, when every instinct in me is prompting me to do otherwise? are powerless to give a satisfactory answer. Confessing no God, they have no room in their vocabulary for the word Ought. But if science, even when mixed with too many foreign ingredients to allow of our speaking of it as "pure," is clearly unequal to the task of telling men in what manner and on what terms they ought to live with one another, how utterly incompetent it must be to instruct them in the right way of living with their God! Christians believe that upon this highest of all subjects intelligence has been received by message. God, they say, has declared his will, and given his commandment; nay, more than this, has to a certain limited extent revealed his purpose. If there have been disclosures in physics, why doubt that there have also been disclosures in ethics? Did Newton's Principia throw any more light on the motions of stars, than Moses in the Decalogue threw upon the relations of souls? Is it not the better conclusion then, that both men were revealers, chosen of God to be such, sent here to tell us new truth? Or, again, take such questions as touch the future, and consider how helpless we are, apart from the aid given us by disclosure. Interesting as is the problem of origins, the problem of destiny is more so. That our tenancy of this planet had a beginning is demonstrable; that it will have an ending is therefore probable; but what sort of an ending? Is there nothing better in store for the round world than the becoming either an ice-pack or a cinder? To this question natural science, as at present informed, says No. But Christians hold that however things may turn out with the globe itself, we who live upon it have received by message certain definite and precious promises, that assure to the family a brighter destiny than awaits the homestead.

In other words, natural science can predict the world's physical future, with a certain measure of accuracy; but religion alone professes to have anything to tell as to the moral and spiritual issues wrapped up with the great fact that an end certainly is to come. Science can prophesy in a sense; there are certain things it can foretell; but if the prophecy is to be translated, the meaning of the writing shown, the real issues determined, a Daniel must be called to judgment, one "in whom is the spirit of the holy Gods," a messenger competent to interpret and to declare.

The whole question, therefore, resolves itself into

one of credentials. Are these voices to which Christians have given assent trustworthy? Can the messengers, the witnesses, the interpreters, call them which you choose, stand the cross-questioning to which the modern spirit is determined to subject all comers who make a claim upon its confidence? We are living in the midst of this cross-questioning process; it is going on before our eyes; the witnesses are under fire; and the world, looking on, abides the result. But you and I cannot afford to sit aside with folded hands, waiting for a verdict that may not be announced at the lips of the learned for a century to come. What are we to do? How are we to settle for ourselves the question of credibility? In precisely the same way, I venture to suggest, that the spectators at an ordinary trial, who are not themselves in the jury box, make up their minds as to the rights and wrongs of the question at issue; namely, by looking the witnesses squarely in the face and forming an independent judgment as to their honesty. In a deeper sense than the poet himself imagined is "full assurance" sometimes "given by looks." It is possible with one's Bible in hand to look Moses, Isaiah, St. John, St. Paul, not to name the holiest of all the names, directly in the eye, and to answer to one's own satisfaction the question, Is this man a deceiver, or do his features bear the stamp of honesty? Even in Old Testament times, uncritical as we are assured those times were, it was customary to subject all who gave themselves forth as messengers of God and unveilers of his mind, to very searching tests. They discriminated carefully between prophets and "false prophets," the men who had the genuine gift of vision and the men who only pretended to have it. "Woe unto the false prophets," vehemently exclaimed one of the true ones, "who follow their own spirit and have seen nothing." Doubtless the method of detecting the false prophets was that simple one which I have called "looking in the face." Insincerity has a way of betraying itself, if not upon the moment, sooner or later. The holy prophets which have been since the world began, have held their own all these centuries, because the successive generations of men have found that good, and only good, came of taking them at their word. To the argument in their favor afforded by the very manner of their speech, has been added the argument which credits a tree with goodness because of the goodness of the fruit; and the two arguments taken together have been very helpful to plain people, as in fact they are likely to continue to be.

But we are told that the time has come when it is fatal to the life of any religion that it should be under the necessity of confessing itself a "book-religion"; and that since this is a confession which Christianity must needs make, the inference necessarily follows that the days of Christianity are numbered. What shall we say to this? First of all, that we are not in the least degree ashamed of making our confession. The fact is as alleged; it is impossible to deny that, for better or for worse, the fortunes of Christ's reli-

chronicle maintained, a record kept. To enable suppliants thus to press God with a major premise, to
urge upon Him old loving-kindnesses as a reason for
bestowing new ones, there must be a memory that
can and does reach far back into the past. Experience cannot be extemporized. The reach even of a
lifetime, if it be a disconnected lifetime, is insuffi-
cient to breed the confidence we hunger after.

The only trustworthy basis on which to build the
fabric of hope is memory, and a far-reaching memory
at that, — "the foundations of many generations."
A religion tangent to human affairs at only one point
is inadequate ; we want one that coheres with all the
past. But such a religion will be from the very necessities of the case a book-religion. If God be indeed
a conscious person who "at sundry times and in
divers manners" has from the beginning been communicating with his creature man, how should we of
this day be at all the better for that fact unless the
word spoken and the deed done had been chronicled ?
But the chronicle, whether it be graven on brass, or
cut in stone, or written on parchment, or printed on
paper, is, to all intents and purposes, the Book.

Moreover, not only are records essential to our
knowing God ; they are equally essential to our knowing man ; and the knowledge of our fellow-man is no
slight part of religion. Records help us to know man
by enlarging the mirror in which we study his reflected image. Nineteenth century man, taken alone,
is not man, he is a mere fragment of man. If we

nervousness or anxiety about going down to the
bottom of things, and calmly considering the question whether the bare fact that the Bible is a book
be or be not fatal to the continuance of the religion
whose book it is.

To charge Christianity with being a book-religion
is only another way of condemning it for being of an
historical character, and having a foothold in the
past. It is the fond conceit of some that a day is
coming when religion will be able to dispense with
documents altogether. Before very long, they hope
to see the matter in such a shape that a few simple
propositions, received on their own merits as self-
evident, and unincumbered by any wearisome appeal
to history, will be accepted as an all-sufficient basis
for the holy life, a trustworthy index of the perfect
way. Why, they ask contemptuously, should faith be
compelled to limp along fettered to a huge volume,
clogged by the weight of ancient chronicles, and bend-
ing beneath a burden of old prophecies hard to be understood ? The remonstrance has a plausible sound,
and for the moment we feel disposed to yield to it,
to throw away the parchments as things not worth
remembering, and to start out with a light heart in
search of this simple and easy religion of the future.

But when we sit down quietly to think the whole
matter over before actually committing ourselves to
this new departure, slowly it begins to dawn on us
that a religion which has nothing to tell about the
past ; which can point to no evidences of the working

of God in history; affects to be beyond the need of way-marks and footprints; acknowledges no epochs of unveiling, no seasons of special vision; cannot say, "There, there, and there He passed, and men felt the breath of his presence as He went by," — it begins to be made plain to us that a religion which can do none of these things, but, instead, boasts of itself as being wholly without records and quite free from such troublesome *impedimenta* as sacred annals, is scarcely a religion we can afford implicitly to trust. A God who is " to everlasting " does not suffice us; we would have one who is " from everlasting " also. The present is of immense importance, but somehow it seems to lose vitality, to become anæmic, when the ligaments that tie it to the past have been cut. If religion were nothing more or better than theosophy, nothing other, that is to say, than an attempt at un-derstanding the inner nature of the Divine Being by dint of blank contemplation, a patient sitting under the fig-tree of pure thought, then, indeed, there might be something to say in behalf of this proposal to break wholly with the past, and to begin afresh, as it were, with a newly-discovered God. But to the mind that is in earnest, to the heart aflame with eager interest to justify the ways of God to man, such a limiting of religion's scope, such a narrowing of her range is most distasteful and ominous. We crave evidence that God has always " from the beginning " taken an interest in the affairs of earth; that the long story of the world's troubles and triumphs has a thread of connection running through it; that the generations have been knit together by a tie of purpose; that events are leading the race up to a definite crisis in the future, for which the whole past has been a preparation; and that the things concerning us men have an end.

This is the meaning of those strong appeals to God in which the Christian Scriptures abound, as the God of the ancient times and of the former peoples; faith in Him as the God of Abraham is strong, but faith in Him as the God of Abraham, of Isaac, and of Jacob is trebly strong. In other words, the argument for belief is cumulative, gathering weight and momentum as the cycles unfold. Listen to David at one of his moments of distress when in the deep waters he is grasping after some bit of floating truth, some fragment of conviction buoyant enough to save him from wholly going under, — "O my God," he cries, " our fathers hoped in thee, they trusted in thee, and thou didst deliver them." He would have been all at sea without the record, the memorandum.

Listen to Solomon at the dedication of the temple gathering up his long supplication into one comprehensive suffrage, — "The Lord our God be with us as He was with our fathers; Let Him not leave us nor forsake us." How came it to be possible for the one monarch in his calamity, and for the other at his supreme hour of triumph, thus to make identically the same appeal to Deity as a "God of the fathers"? Clearly because a tradition had been handed on, a chronicle maintained, a record kept. To enable suppliants thus to press God with a major premise, to urge upon Him old loving-kindnesses as a reason for bestowing new ones, there must be a memory that can and does reach far back into the past. Experience cannot be extemporized. The reach even of a lifetime, if it be a disconnected lifetime, is insufficient to breed the confidence we hunger after.

The only trustworthy basis on which to build the fabric of hope is memory, and a far-reaching memory at that, — " the foundations of many generations." A religion tangent to human affairs at only one point is inadequate ; we want one that coheres with all the past. But such a religion will be from the very necessities of the case a book-religion. If God be indeed a conscious person who " at sundry times and in divers manners " has from the beginning been communicating with his creature man, how should we of this day be at all the better for that fact unless the word spoken and the deed done had been chronicled ? But the chronicle, whether it be graven on brass, or cut in stone, or written on parchment, or printed on paper, is, to all intents and purposes, the Book.

Moreover, not only are records essential to our knowing God ; they are equally essential to our knowing man ; and the knowledge of our fellow-man is no slight part of religion. Records help us to know man by enlarging the mirror in which we study his reflected image. Nineteenth century man, taken alone, is not man, he is a mere fragment of man. If we

would know man in his entirety we must study
him in every ascertainable stage of his existence.
The cave-dweller whose likeness was opportunely
scratched for us on a bit of reindeer horn, the Egyptian whose profile we know from wall paintings as old
as Thebes, the Assyrian warrior pushing on his char-
iot of stone and horses of stone against the stone
enemy he can never overtake, — these people have a
kinship with us as real as theirs who looked down on
us from the walls of last year's Salon.

But, it may be asked, why not prosecute this study
of man as he shows himself from China to Peru, and
as he has shown himself from the first day until
now ; in the pages of the so-called secular historians?
Why should Biblical annalists be accounted especially
valuable in such an undertaking? Are not a Gibbon
and a Hallam as helpful as a Moses and an Ezra? To
which the proper reply would seem to be, This ought
ye to have done and not to leave the other undone.
Doubtless all history is rich in the materials of a true
anthropology. But the noticeable characteristic of
the Bible writers is that they, in a unique sense, have
given us the biography of the human conscience. The
Greek tragedians can perhaps be said to come near
them in this line, but it is only with an occasional
approach. In what we know as " Holy Scripture,"
and in that only of all the literatures of the earth,
man walks ever either in the approving or the condemning presence of a watchful Judge. In these
chronicles heaven's verdict is pronounced on every

mortal career with passionless precision. We are not deceived by false epithets as in popular histories. Jezebel is not named " the Fair," nor Herod styled " the Great." The fact that " he did evil in the sight of the Lord " constitutes in these pages the condemnation of a king, no matter how much he may have added to the national territory or advanced the credit of the tribes. Next in importance to the definite announcements of fact, to which I have already referred as making the true *differentia* of the Bible, ought to be reckoned this pervasive flavor of righteousness. Other sacred books contain in abundance what we know as religious sentiment, vague aspiration, pathetic unrest, the consciousness of insignificance, the sense of mystery; the Bible alone insists on knowing, first of all, whether the heart of the devotee be set on doing the thing that is right.

Looked at as the literature of a people the Scriptures have certainly much in common with other literatures. There is poetry there, there is history, there is biography, there is mental philosophy, there is drama, there is correspondence, there are the pithy sayings into which a people's mind condenses its wise conclusions, there is impassioned eloquence, there is allegory, there are confessions, there are forecastings of the future, there are commentaries upon the past, there is a book of laws and there is a book of psalms. Kings move across the pages; soldiers and armies are in motion hither and thither, courtiers and nobles, laboring men and peasants, women, maidens, children,

— all are there, coming and going. Sometimes the scene lies in the city, sometimes in the fields, sometimes the background is of woods and mountains. But even so are all great national literatures fashioned. Into every one of them enter these component parts. Across the field of each marches and countermarches the like procession. How then differs the Bible from them all ? What is that distinguishing note or mark by means of which we distinguish *the* Book from all books beside ? It is the presence throughout the Scriptures of what we may call the flavor of righteousness. These sacred writers, as they are properly named, all of them look at life and at the earth's various history from a single standpoint ; they are critics of conduct; they not only narrate, they judge.

It is, indeed, conceivable that men may one day rise up and banish religion in every form and shape from the earth, sometimes it looks as if they were really meaning to do that; but if religion is to stay with us, the Bible, simply by dint of its surpassing spiritual vigor, and for lack of any adequate competitor, is certain to outlive all rivals. The ethnic scriptures have become easily accessible within recent years, they are to be found in English translations on the shelves of all well-appointed public libraries, and it is possible for anybody to institute on his own account such a comparison as I have suggested. Look for yourselves into the sacred books of Brahmins, Buddhists, and Confucians, and see whether anywhere you catch the peculiar quality of voice, at once mandatory and persuasive, so easily audible in our own Scriptures. Where in them do we find anything that strikes home to the conscience with the sturdy strength that lives in the arm of Moses, man of God, or lies back of the well-aimed blow of Paul, soldier and servant of Jesus Christ? Many bitter things have been said about the Bible, first and last, by those who have had a grudge against it; but no one, so far as I know, has ever ventured upon calling it a weak book. Virility penetrates every page of it; for any slightest trace of feebleness or sentimentality we search the Scriptures to no purpose; it is not there.

To strength add delicacy. The Bible writers are not only of stalwart breed, they show everywhere what we may call religious refinement, a certain sensitiveness of retina in the matter of discerning nice shades of spiritual difference. Let the student of comparative religion match if he can the dignity of the Psalms; the clear-voiced witness of the greater and the lesser prophets against the materialism of their times; the lucid simplicity of speech in which St. John, the eagle of the Evangelists, tells the story of the Word made flesh.

But most of all, and with carefulest search, let him try whether he can find elsewhere anything resembling the Bible's guarantee of forgiveness and promise of eternal life. Here we come back to what I have already emphasized as the announcements of Scripture. With trifling exceptions, the parables of Nature make strongly against belief in the forgiveness of sins, and are subversive of " the blessed hope of everlasting life." The Bible, with a voice of authority, speaks to us and gives assurance of both pardon and immortality. Here is the secret of the book's perpetuity ; live it must, because of the good news in it. Men's hearts are not so rich in hope that they can willingly, or for any long time, shut their ears against the only message annunciatory of better things to come that has ever yet commanded and held the assent of any considerable number of minds acknowledged great.

Do not understand me as wishing to cast the slightest slur upon what is praiseworthy in the sacred books of the heathen peoples. In order to prove our own Scriptures invaluable, it is not necessary to declare all other Scriptures valueless. Goodness and truth, wherever we find them, and in whatever measure, are of God, and whenever we discover their presence, we are bound to acknowledge their origin. We have St. Paul's warrant for believing that the heathen have not been left wholly without witness, so far as concerns one of the gravest interests of religion, moral responsibility ; and doubtless not a few rays of the light which lighteth " every man," may be found garnered in the Scriptures of faiths other than ours. But voluntarily and gratuitously to propose to exchange our daylight for their twilight is to flatter the heathen overmuch. Our safety does not lie in eclecticism. Not by any piecing together of fragments of religions, not by picking up a pebble here and a pebble there, as artists in mosaic make their pictures, are we to find our portraiture of the God and Father of us all. No matching of selected features gathered from all faiths, however ingeniously put together, will ever work a displacement of the likeness already accepted by the Christian conscious-ness as true, so manifestly does the Bible picture of the Divine Majesty surpass all competing attempts to show us what God is like. The Christian Evidence Societies could do the public no better service than to print for purposes of contrast an edition, say, of the Gospel of St. John, interleaved with the very best sentences it is possible to gather from the sacred lit-eratures of the East. The whole controversy would, in that case, be condensed into a simple " Look here upon this picture, and on this."

So far as we have as yet developed it, the argument may be put into three sentences. First, the world cannot live, at least cannot live contentedly, without religion. Secondly, religion cannot live, at least can-not adequately live, without records, without an authenticated history, a book of words and acts. Thirdly, among such books, and they are many, the Christian Scriptures, even by the confession of un-friendly critics, stand supreme.

I pass now to consider the function of criticism with respect to the Scriptures, and the construction that ought to be put upon the words Inspiration and Revelation. It is obvious to remark that without what we understand by criticism we never should have had the Bible in its present shape at all. Criticism is the exercise of discernment; as an instrument it may be likened to the flail. The critic essays to separate the more from the less precious, and to tell us why he does so. In some instances criticism is the work of an individual, sometimes of a deliberative body supposed to be composed of qualified judges; and sometimes, again, it is the slow action of a public opinion that makes itself heard in only half articulate ways, and at odd intervals, but still does, sooner or later, carry its point and hold the field.

Beginners in theology are apt to be very much disturbed in mind because nobody can give them a hard and fast account of the precise manner in which the canon of the Old Testament and the canon of the New were originally determined. The instinct in us that craves precision is piqued when it is discovered that, in an important inquiry, day and date are missing. It is well known that in the early Church there were differences of opinion with respect to the limits of the canon. There were certain books universally received; there were certain others open to challenge. In some congregations lessons were read from the Shepherd of Hermas, for example, a Scripture with which at present only patristic students are familiar. How was it ever brought to pass that there did finally emerge the collection we now have as the New Testament? An intelligent believer will be likely to answer the question thus, The result was brought to pass under the oversight of Almighty God by the instrumentality of criticism.

The criticism was doubtless exercised by all three of the methods I just named. Solitary scholars, each man working by himself, had part in it; councils of bishops had part in it; public opinion, declaring itself in all sorts of unclassified ways, had part in it. Finally, as the result of the best judgment of the times there came forth the collection as we have it; the canon, as we say, was closed. A not wholly dissimilar process gave us, in the region of secular literature, what we know as " the classics." It is impossible to say precisely who assorted the ancient authors, and decided just which should be and which should not be accounted classical. All the same we have the classics ; that they exist is an unquestionable fact; no one can shut his eyes to their presence in literature ; they are here. Moreover, the fact is one that is not at all imperilled by the confessed possibility of error on the part of those who originally determined the metes and bounds of classicality. Because the right of this or that obscure poet of post-Augustan times to a place among the Latin classics may happen to be disputed, no one trembles for Catullus or for Virgil. The *Amen* of many generations has given sanction to the list as a whole, and though modern criticism may nibble at the edges of the codex, the substance remains.

We ought to be equally confident with respect to

the classics of religion, the Scriptures of the Old and
New Testaments. Through aid of criticism they were
originally marked off from other Scriptures, and iso-
lated as having in them a certain distinctive something not elsewhere to be found. If criticism did us
this good service some seventeen or eighteen hundred
years ago, why look askance at criticism when it
comes in nineteenth century guise proposing to re-
open questions of authorship and canonicity in connection with our sacred books? It may be urged
against this way of looking at the matter that since
it has pleased God to shroud the beginnings of many
beneficent growths, that of the State, for instance, in
darkness, a reverent prudence would discountenance
any attempt to investigate the beginnings of the Bible.
The remonstrance has a certain measure of reason-
ableness in it, and deserves a hearing; to sneer at it
as childish is more easy than wise. Doubtless it is, in
a sense, calamitous for society when the analytical
fit seizes it, and all life comes to be written over
with interrogation marks. There is a sickly as well as
a healthy curiosity, and that is by no means the best
horticulture which is for ever bent on pulling things
up by the roots with the professed object of seeing
how they began. On the compiler of every document
that in any measure is expected to bind posterity, be
it constitution, code, or canon, a specially solemn responsibility rests of doing what is to be done in such
a workmanlike manner that there will be slight need
of revision. Particularly in matters that touch the

conscience is it desirable that the presumption should be as strong as possible in favor of things as they are, and against the needless re-investigation of origins. It is better to keep the Ten Commandments as they stand, than to become so deeply versed in the methods of ethics as to be doubtful whether the keeping them or the breaking them makes very much difference in the end.

But while all this is true, it is equally indisputable that occasions do arise when the reinvestigation of beginnings is imperative. A man whose house is on the river's bank may live in it for years without a moment's uneasiness; but if by and by his neighbors come to him, one after another, with the alarming statement that the current is wearing away his foundations, he is a fool if he refuses to allow an expert to investigate the matter. He may personally feel very sure that the neighbors are mistaken, and that no real danger threatens; nevertheless, if it be only to set the mind of the community at rest, and to quiet the clamor, he will do well not merely to allow but to encourage investigation. The principle holds good not of houses only but of treasures of all sorts; the owners of family diamonds who are afraid to submit them to the judgment of the lapidary, the coiner who shrinks from letting the sharp acid touch his gold, are persons of doubtful wealth. There is a certain holy intrepidity which thorough-going believers are bound to cultivate. If the Bible have in it, as Christians hold, an authentic message from heaven to earth, there is no corrosive known to scholarship that can eat away the substance of it. When our Lord Jesus Christ said " Search the Scriptures," he gave biblical criticism its everlasting warrant.

The practical question, therefore, is this : Are present circumstances such as make a reinvestigation of the whole matter desirable ? A great company of thoughtful and not undevout people are saying Yes; and whether they are right or wrong, more harm is likely to come of trying to prevent their having their way, than can possibly accrue from cordially letting them have it, and starting them with a *Bon voyage*. It is impossible that the friends of God should really have anything to fear from what an honest scholarship may attempt; and that man, I do not hesitate to affirm, who happens to be to-day the one who is doing the most to throw white light upon the things written in the Bible has better right than any other living to be entitled Defender of the Faith.

A little more than fifty years ago, Arnold of Rugby predicted the crisis in the midst of which we find ourselves. "Have you seen," he wrote to his friend Mr. Justice Coleridge, " your uncle's ' Letters on Inspiration,' which I believe are to be published ? They are well fitted to break ground in the approaches to that momentous question which involves in it so great a shock to existing notions; the greatest, probably, that has ever been given since the discovery of the falsehood of the doctrine of the Pope's infallibility. Yet it must come; and will end, in spite of the fears and clamors of the weak and bigoted, in the higher exalting and more sure establishing of Christian truth."

So spoke a true prophet, little dreaming of the parts a son and a granddaughter of his own were destined to play in the commotion he foresaw.

The "existing notions" to which Arnold referred were doubtless such as had to do with the nature and methods of inspiration. That the words of Scripture had been actually dictated, syllable by syllable, to the writers of the several books by a voice from without themselves; that for the purposes of composition evangelists and apostles had been, to use the cant of spiritualism, simply "trance mediums," unconscious of what they did, — this was the notion upon which the disciple of Niebuhr and the friend of Whately felt sure that doom had been pronounced. No one whose eyes are open to the movements of contemporary thought can fail to see that the revolution predicted is in progress. It is no longer held or taught by intelligent theologians anywhere that the writers of the books of the Bible were mere amanuenses, no more personally accountable for their words than the automaton chess-player for his moves. On the contrary, these authors are acknowledged to have been such in the proper sense of the word. They are spoken of as compilers; they are compared one with another in respect to the facilities they severally enjoyed for gathering accurate information; each is recognized as having his own proper literary style, and, in matters where temper and spirit come in, his own personal equation.

But because our estimate of the scope and manner of inspiration has been modified, does it follow that our faith in the Bible as a *bona fide* message from God must suffer shipwreck? By no means. When we think of it we see that it is impossible for any book, no matter how sacred, to be inspired. Only that which has life can breathe, and breath enters into the very definition of inspiration. It is men who are inspired, not books; prophets and saints who breathe in the truth of God, not the papyrus or the wax which serve them as their instruments of transmission. The familiar phrase "the inspiration of the Bible" must, therefore, in order to become intelligible, be expanded into the inspiration of the men who wrote the Bible. The evidence that the men who wrote the Bible were, as a matter of fact, breathed into by Almighty God in such a way as to give to what they wrote a value wholly unique, is to be sought for in the characteristics of the book taken as a whole, and in the history of what it has done for the peoples which have accepted it as trustworthy.

Of the characteristics of the Bible over and above those that have been already emphasized, by far the most striking is its unity. The book is symmetrical and self-consistent to a wonderful degree. I am aware that symmetry is sometimes an accidental product. If I throw a thousand handfuls of sand successively upon the floor, it may happen in one instance out of the thousand that the particles will be found arranged in such a manner as to suggest a set pattern. But the impression produced on the mind by this result is very different from that which follows from seeing the grains of sand sprinkled over the surface of a metallic disk arrange themselves in a particular geometrical shape in response to the particular note of sound that has set the disk to vibrating. In this instance we recognize a symmetry intentionally brought to pass by the experimentalist, who knew before striking the note just what result would follow. I do not assert that the evidence of unity of plan afforded by the symmetry of the Bible, is such as to be overwhelmingly demonstrative. I do say that to many minds it has commended itself as singularly persuasive.

Had the Scriptures all of them been written within a year or within ten years, or even within a single generation, there would be nothing wonderful about their possessing unity of plan. In the case of a book like the Koran the wonder is that it has not more symmetry than it has. But we are to remember that in the case of the Bible, the dates of the authorship of the various parts differ by centuries, and we must reckon at least sixteen hundred years to get the span of the whole arch.

Clearly the most reasonable hypothesis upon which to account for the Bible's symmetry, granting that it exists, is the supposition of an extraneous guidance that moved the authors in such manner, and with such force, as to make all of them co-operant to a common end. For such providential guidance, supplied from above, there can be no better name than inspiration, — that inbreathing of a more enlightened spirit than man's own, whereby he is enabled to "think those things that are good."

But more to the point by far than "inspiration" is the allied word "revelation." What we really want to know is whether the Bible writers do actually unveil to us certain facts of grave moment which we could never know but for such help. The matters to which I refer are such as these, the personality of God, the pre-existence of Jesus Christ, man's survival of death, the prospect of an ultimate restitution of all things, the reality of heaven, the reality of hell ; these are points with respect to which centuries of philosophizing can help us not one whit. If such truths, supposing them to be truths, are to be known at all, they must become known by a drawing aside of the curtain ; no otherwise is it conceivable that we should become aware of them. The study of Nature and of the human mind may furnish illustrations, and what may even be charitably construed as corroborative evidence, of the matters thus disclosed ; but to disclose them it is powerless. The logical mind is shut up to a choice between Pyrrhonism and revelation.

The advantage gained by shifting the burden of argument from inspiration to revelation is further evident when we consider that inspiration is a thing of degrees, a matter of more and less, whereas, with respect to revelation all we have to ask is, Has it or has it not occurred? There is a sense of the word in which inspiration is credited to all men who accomplish more than the common. Bezaleel is said in the Book of Exodus to have been filled with the Spirit of God "to work in gold and in silver and in brass, and in cutting of stones to set them, and in carving of timber." This is a definition of inspiration large enough to cover the case of Leonardo da Vinci, the Bezaleel of the Renaissance. So then, if Christians confine themselves to a claim of "inspiration" for the authors of Scripture, they may find men putting the Bible on the same shelf with other sacred books, wedging it in between Plato and Confucius, and quite content to claim for Isaiah and St. Paul only such a measure of the Spirit as they are willing to concede to Dante, Bunyan, and à-Kempis. A revelation, on the other hand, does not admit of degrees. Either it has been made or it has not been made; either the heavens have been opened and God has showed us the truth, or they are brass over our head for ever.

To a mind studying the Bible from the point of approach now indicated, many of the so-called difficulties of faith shrink into insignificance. The intimation, for example, of little inaccuracies in the record, whether of an historical, a geographical, or a scientific sort, cease to alarm. Are the great structural lines of the whole fabric right and true? is the real question. Because I accept the erratum of some chronologist who has discovered a wrong date in the Books of Chronicles, it does not follow that I am logically bound to welcome with open arms a whole troop of interpreters who are bent on writing the Resurrection down a myth, and distilling the personality of God into a figure of speech. Let every proposition be tried on its own merits, and, above all, let us distinguish magnitudes. We are never really the poorer for having been told the truth ; but we are sometimes frightened into taking for true, statements contradictory to cherished beliefs, when really it is the new announcement rather than the old faith that lacks verification. We do not the less enjoy the glories of the sunset because it has been discovered that the going down of the sun means really the backing around of the earth ; but every now and then credulous people are thrown into a paroxysm of alarm by some pseudo-scientific announcement that a great cosmic disturbance is impending. There is a difference in the two cases. In like manner, if I am asked to give up the Bible as the Word of God because Solomon, reputed the wisest of men and inspired, was certainly mistaken when he spoke of the clouds as dropping down the dew, and probably mistaken in what he said about the habits of ants, I decline to be so foolish as to let my heart fail me on any such grounds. My confidence in the Bible as an authentic unfolding of the truth, the will, and the purposes of God has anchorage deeper down.

The simple fact of the matter is this ; modern re-

search is modifying, — some say revolutionizing, but
it is more accurate to say modifying, old opinions as
to the process by which the various books of the
Bible were brought into their present combination,
and made into the volume as we have it now. Modern research, be it also observed, is doing what it is
doing after a fashion not unlike that in which Sedg-
wick, Murchison, and Lyell changed our old conceptions of the manner in which the globe was brought
to be what to-day it is. But the earth itself is precisely what it was before the geologists began to
investigate, and the book we know as the Bible is
precisely what it was before the critics began to criticise. And just as there are those of us who while
thankfully accepting all that Geology can really prove
with respect to the formation of the earth's crust,
nevertheless hold fast the old-fashioned faith which
expresses itself in the words, "I believe in God, the
Father Almighty, Maker;" so there are those of us,
and their number is reckoned by tens of thousands,
who while ready cheerfully to concede whatever the
best critical scholarship may be able to establish
regarding the formation of the Scriptures as an historical process, are not at all shaken in their
confidence that as the record of God's revelation of
Himself, the Bible, substantially as we have it now,
will stand to the end of time.

What I mean is that the man must be either of a
singularly sanguine temperament, or else strangely
forgetful of the oscillations of scholarship in the past,

who fancies that the books of the Bible will ever be, by general consent, redistributed and renamed to suit the conclusions of contemporary criticism. All sorts of theories may, from time to time, be set afloat as to the proper chronological order of the volume's component parts, and these theories may make converts many and distinguished, but the volume itself will continue, as at present, to begin with the book called Genesis and to end with the book called Revelation. To the eye of criticism Jehovist and Elohist may grow to seem more distinctly separable than ever, but like flies in amber the two will continue to maintain their twin existence in the narrative as at this day. It is unlikely, in other words, that any scheme for remodelling the whole structure of the Bible will ever get beyond the academic stage. The thing may be discussed and urged, but the moment action becomes imminent a still more recent scholarship will step in to affirm that, if change there is to be, it should proceed on lines different from those proposed. In saying this I am not charging scholarship with fickleness, I am merely calling attention to the fact that in the field of Biblical science absolute demonstration is unattainable, and to the probability that since such is the case, no one hypothesis will ever so effectually distance all the others that the maintainers of it will be allowed to reconstruct the canon at their pleasure. The argument against the authenticity of II. Peter, for example, and the argument in favor of the multiple authorship of Isaiah may both of them become in the future very much stronger than they are to-day, but it is in the highest degree unlikely that such a complete consensus of critical opinion will ultimately be secured as to warrant, say, the Syndics of the University Press in dropping the one book and in subdividing the other.

Not only so, but when it comes to fretting ourselves over the detection of petty errors and faults in the text of Scripture, we shall do well to re-read our Butler, and having got ourselves thoroughly into the spirit of the Analogy to make note of the singular fact that none of the creations of God as we observe them in the outer world are perfect, according to our human conceptions and definitions of perfectness. Of man it has been truly said,

> "The type of perfect in his mind
> In Nature can he nowhere find."

Why stumble then at discovering in the Book of Revelation a characteristic equally discernible in the Book of Nature, supposing the two books to have had one and the same author? Who, for instance, ever saw an absolutely flawless petal on a stem? But do we, for that reason, doubt God's having made the roses? A draughtsman with a pencil and a ruler can, in a few moments, plot for us on paper an outline of the perfect hexagonal prism which is the ideal form of a quartz crystal,— the form in which, as we say (greatly presuming in saying so), that quartz "ought" to crystallize. But we may search the quarries and grottoes of the world in vain for any bit of actual quartz that shall conform absolutely and without the slightest deviation to the draughtsman's pattern. Are we to assume for this reason that the draughtsman has a better mind than God ? or account the hand which can draw so easily the lines of an ideal crystal defter than the Hand which has been shaping the real crystal through uncounted ages ? Not if we have weighed well the purport of that ancient challenge, — " He that made the eye, shall He not see ? " Scarcely enough seems to have been made of this particular argument from analogy in recent apologetics. For if we find what look to our eye blemishes in workmanship which we know to be wholly God's, such as the flowers and the rocks, ought we to be troubled at discovering the like signs and tokens to be characteristic of a book in the making of which God may be said to have taken man into partnership? Why not have the good sense to look at the Bible as we look at everything else that has been subject to the necessary conditions of life and growth, and not let the knees of our faith knock together in alarm the moment this or that student of the text points out to us some fleck or flaw, as he is pleased to think it, in the workmanship of Almighty God ? Some lynx-eyed Old Testament critic assures me, with the air of a Samson pulling down the temple, that he has discovered a discrepancy between a certain statement in the Book of Leviticus and a certain other statement in the Book of Deuteronomy.

First of all, I ask him whether he is quite sure that he is right; but even when convinced that his discovery is genuine, I decline to feel as seriously concerned over it as he would like to have me feel. If God has seen fit to inject his revelation into the midst of human affairs, I am not surprised to find the history of it subject to the same disabilities that attach to ordinary history. "I adore," says Athenagoras, "the Being who harmonized the strains and leads the melody, not the instrument which he plays. What umpires at the games, omitting to crown the minstrel, place the garland upon the lyre."

The Bible, as we know it to-day, is an accomplished fact, and what it is it is. It stands out before us like a great tree that has attained its growth. As such it has a complete contour of its own, and we might as well attempt to kill a tree by criticism as hope to make away with the Bible by philosophizing on the method and order of its growth. On a sunny slope in an English nobleman's park, flourishing far away from the country and climate of its birth, we find a stately, heavy-foliaged cedar, one of those great "trees of the Lord" of which the Psalmists tell, the pride of Lebanon. English soil of itself never could have produced the tree; the land in which it first had root and from which it was transplanted is the land of Palestine, the land called "Holy." But is it here and now any the less the cedar, any the less "tree of Jehovah" on that account? Does the fact of its being an exotic destroy its beauty or its value? No, it is as much a tree of God's planting in England as ever it could have been in Syria. We notice, here and there upon the trunk, gnarled spots that tell of an irregular growth, and betray some past departure from the normal movement of the juices within. Is it the less a cedar, the less worthy to be called God's tree for that reason ? At the extremity of one of the limbs there happens to be a dead branch ; it suggests curious thoughts. Why did that particular branch wither ? All the adjoining foliage is quick and beautiful and fresh as ever; why should that one outermost shred of the tree's vesture thus have shrivelled ? Did disease attack it from within, or has some blight struck it from without ? We cannot tell ; we are as much perplexed as we were by the flaws on the rough surface of the bark. But what of that ? Do we for a moment distrust the venerable cedar, question its genuineness, deny its authenticity ? No ; we look at it with reverent awe ; we glory in it just as it is ; we say, — Truly it is the Lord's tree, all the marks of his undoubted workmanship are here ; it is Jehovah's cedar ; He made it. Under the shadow of the branches I will lay me down and take my rest."

Our answer then to the question, How ought men in these times to think about the Bible ? so far as the positive side of the Anglican statement is concerned, should be this. We ought to account the Bible to be the permanent hand-book of authentic religion, — a hand-book open always to new and larger interpretations as fast as human knowledge widens, a hand-book which scholars must be permitted to criticise and re-edit with the same absolute freedom with which they criticise and re-edit the text of the secular classics, but a hand-book destined to continue substantially what it is to-day until the end of the age, still, as of old, the Word of God to man.

But before this question of the Scriptures is wholly left behind, something ought to be said with reference to the alleged insufficiency of the Bible as a repository of religious truth. Attention has thus far been engrossed with the arguments of the left, but what the Bishops have to say upon this subject is also open to attack from the extreme right. Roman Catholics take the ground that the Scriptures unsupplemented by something more are inadequate, that they are good as far as they go, but that they do not go far enough.

This theory of a duplex revelation has been succinctly stated thus : " Every sort of doctrine which is to be delivered to the faithful is contained in the Word of God, which is divided into Scripture and Tradition."[1] That tradition has been by most Protestant controversialists greatly undervalued, is doubtless true. In matters secular we could ill afford to spare knowledge that has come down to us in all sorts of informal and irregular and unauthenticated ways. Even so precise a thing as statute law demands of its interpreter some acquaintance with old uses and time-worn consent, with the things that " go without saying." We should consider the historian foolish who based his account

---

[1] Catechism of Council of Trent, Preface, Qu. xii.

of a people's beginnings wholly upon folk-lore, with the
expectation of having what he wrote considered trustworthy, but on the other hand to rule out the folk-lore
altogether would be almost as great a folly. It would
be unsafe to assume, for instance, that the Arthurian
legend had no grain of truth in it; and though the hero
of the Robin Hood ballads may never have existed, the
ballads themselves certainly throw light on the manners and customs, the popular loves and hatreds of
Norman England.

If the Roman Catholic would be content to treat
tradition as illustrative, and not insist on our receiving it as demonstrative, we should have no quarrel with him. The Church of England avails itself of
tradition as a side-light when in the preface to its
Ordinal it calls in "ancient authors" to buttress by
their testimony the Scriptural argument for Episcopacy. Most Anglicans are also glad to take up with
such help as tradition has to give in the matter of infant
baptism, and the transference of the Sabbatical sanction from the last to the first day of the week. And
yet, on the other hand, it ought carefully to be observed
that the Church of England has nowhere given to any
one of these contentions the dignity of an article of
the faith. The statement, "The baptism of young
children is in any wise to be retained in the Church,
as most agreeable with the institution of Christ,"[1] is
not put upon a level with the statement, "The third
day He rose again from the dead."

[1] Article xxvii.

Acceptance of the belief that "from the Apostles' time there have been these orders of ministers in Christ's Church, Bishops, Priests, and Deacons," is not made a prerequisite to receiving the Holy Communion. Only to such propositions as she has held, whether rightly or wrongly, to be demonstrably scriptural, has the Church of England ever demanded the assent of all her children.[1]

The necessity of taking this rigid attitude towards tradition, if a religion is to be kept pure, is occasioned by the fecundity that inheres in tradition by the very nature of the thing. The Bible piques as well as gratifies our curiosity. To one question that it answers, it raises a dozen which it leaves unanswered. The curious mind of man cannot let these unsolved problems alone; in fact, they are all the more fascinating for having been left unsolved. The interest in the Sibylline books that were bought must have been as nothing compared with the longing desire to know what had been on the pages of the burned volumes. And as demand creates supply, so is there great danger that in proportion to the weight with which the silence of Scripture presses on the mind, will be the effort of self-evolving tradition to make good the deficiency. This has to be acknowledged on all hands in the case of the elder revelation. We have it upon the authority of Christ Himself, that in his day the Word of God had been "made of none effect," stifled, He seems to have

[1] Article viii.

meant, by the traditions. It is the old story of the sleeping beauty in the wood. He who comes to seek must cut his way through "bur and brake and briar," before he finds himself even at the door of the enchanted palace.

A clever Mohammedan writer[1] has lately told us that the same thing holds good of Islam.

"You read the Koran," he says, "and you think you know Islamism. That is a great mistake. . . . Besides the Koran, there are traditions which are as powerful and even more respected than the Koran itself. It is difficult for a European to know these traditions. The whole science of Asia, everything which is good or useful, has been attributed to Islam. It is an ocean where you can find everything which is good to be known; and it offers all kinds of facilities, not in the Koran alone, but in the traditions, for the progress of the people."

This liability to overgrowth which neither Judaism nor Islam has been able to escape, attaches to Christianity as well. Nor need the liability be greatly deprecated or deplored so long as the traditions pass for what they are worth and for no more. It is only through gross carelessness on the part of custodians, that the ivy and the lichen ever become the destroyers of the masonry they adorn. There is a great deal that is beautiful in the life of the Church for which it would be difficult to find explicit Scripture warrant. It was narrow of the Puritans to think

[1] Prince Malcolm Khan.

that no names were good enough for Christian children but Bible names; and it is silly of the ultra-
Protestant of our own day to demand a " proof text"
for every pious usage that former generations have
handed on. But it is neither narrow nor silly to insist that when it comes to the ascertainment of the
essentials of our religion, regard shall be had only
to what stands unmistakably on record. Text and
margin are separable things, and should be kept
apart.

III.

THE CREDENDA.

The older I grew, the smaller stress I laid on those controversies and curiosities (though still my intellect abhorreth confusion), as finding greater uncertainties in them than I at first discovered, and finding less usefulness where there is the greatest certainty. The Creed, the Lord's Prayer, and the Ten Commandments are now to me as my daily bread and drink, and as I can speak and write over them again and again, so I had rather read and hear of them than of any of the school niceties. And this I observed also with Richard Hooker and with many other men. — RICHARD BAXTER.

I have found in this way the preciousness of the simple creeds of antiquity, the inward witness which a Gospel of facts possesses, and which a Gospel of notions must always want; how the most awful and absolute truths, which notions displace or obscure, are involved in facts and through facts, may be entertained and embraced by those who do not possess the faculty of comparing notions, and have a blessed incapacity of resting in them. — F. D. MAURICE.

No sober-minded man will hold an opinion against reason, no Christian against Scripture, no lover of peace against the Church. — ST. AUGUSTINE.

III.

THE CREDENDA.

No memorandum of the first principles of Church Unity is complete that leaves dogma wholly out of the account. Men cannot act in concert without *credenda*, and since Christianity, looked at as a great movement for the betterment of human life, of necessity demands concert of action, of necessity also *credenda* it must have. Aware of this, the Bishops at Lambeth assembled set forth, under the head of dogma, "*The Apostles' Creed, as the Baptismal Symbol; and the Nicene Creed, as the sufficient statement of the Christian Faith.*"

We shall be the better able to appreciate the strength of this position if, first of all, some thought be given to the manner in which dogma, as such, stands related to religion. It may be objected that this is a question for the schools, and for the schools only; but the days of the discipline of the secret are ended. Theology can no longer rest content with sitting, in pillared seclusion, far away from the common resorts of men. The other sciences have quitted their academic retirement and have come out into the open. Queen of them though she be, Theology has

no choice but to do as they have done, or run the risk
of being thought to have abdicated her sovereignty.
In these democratic days queens who are only such *in
posse* make a poor showing. I venture therefore upon
a definition, and ask you to think of a dogma as a
statement set forth, either by an individual teacher or
by some teaching body, to be taken for true, while
confessedly not susceptible of logical demonstration.

It is evident that, as thus defined, dogmas are by
no means the exclusive possession of the Christian
Church. Pure science employs dogma very sparingly,
but the mixed sciences are tolerant of it in large
measure. Geometry, for example, a pure science,
makes use of dogma under the name of the " postulate ; " the postulate being an unproved assertion, the
taking of which for granted facilitates the proof of
other things, and thus by a sort of retroaction justifies itself. Nevertheless, Geometry, as a rule, is
shy of dogma, and deals for the most part with what
is directly provable. Not so Biology, and the mixed
sciences in general ; — here dogma abounds, commonly veiled under the name of "working hypothesis." The so-called "law " of natural selection is an
instance in point. No one alleges that natural selection has been demonstrated, or is demonstrable ;
nevertheless, it is taught, and taught with much positiveness, by those who hold it. In fact, to question
this particular working hypothesis brings down upon
the questioner in some quarters censure as sharp, if
not as heavy, as that which in old times fell to the lot

of those who disparaged the dogmas of the Church.
Politics also and Sociology are full of dogma. The
proposition " Universal suffrage makes for the good
of a free people " is a dogma. The nation to which
we belong sets it forth as a thing to be believed, although nobody pretends that it is susceptible of proof.
It is an American dogma. The different schools of
medicine again set forth dogma almost without stint.
There is, for example, the antiseptic dogma, and over
against it the aseptic; the very fact of the co-exist-
ence of the two dogmas being of itself evidence that
neither the antiseptic nor the aseptic hypothesis admits of absolute proof. Should proof be ultimately
forthcoming, the dogma that triumphed would thence-
forth cease to be dogma, having become transmuted
into verified fact. Meanwhile, nevertheless, the sur-
geons, whether of the antiseptic or the aseptic way of
thinking, do not scruple to go on practising in accordance with that one of the two dogmatic bases to
which they the more incline.

But if the thing itself be so obvious a necessity of
human thought and life, how, one may very naturally
ask, has the name for the thing come to incur the
odium which, as all must own, attaches to it?

An easy way of answering the question would be to
attribute the unpopularity of religious dogma directly
to the hardness of men's hearts, to their obstinate
determination to stay in the dark when the choice of
walking in the light is offered them. But of the most
intensely dogmatic teacher that ever trod the earth,

it is written that "the common people heard Him gladly." He taught as one having authority, that is to say, dogmatically, and the multitude followed Him all the more gladly on that account. It is therefore only reasonable to suppose that some portion at least of the disfavor in which dogma has come to be held is a deserved disfavor, the unpopularity an unpopularity merited and earned.

We shall be strengthened in this conviction if we consider two or three of the ways in which the principle of dogma has been abused, wounded in the house of its friends. There has been, for instance, a strong disposition always, on the part of opinionated men, to set forth their own private notions upon all sorts of subjects, as if, instead of being notions, they were decrees. A dogma, like a projectile, has momentum in proportion to the amount and strength of the explosive back of it. When a toy pistol is fired off with all the pomp and circumstance that usually attend the discharge of a three-hundred pounder, the lookers-on smile, they cannot help it. The dogmatist in this way does dogma more harm in a sentence than he can undo in a volume; for the thought of authority enters into all our conceptions of dogma, and for a personal utterance to carry authority the man who makes it must convince us either that he is inspired of some intelligence higher than the human, or that he is an expert in the department in which he undertakes to instruct us, or else that he is the mouth-piece of a very considerable number of consenting minds. Whoever ventures dogmatically to address us simply in his capacity of brother-man makes himself ridiculous, and does what he can to make dogma as such ridiculous also.

But not only have individuals brought discredit upon dogma by their misuse of the dogmatic method, churches are in the same condemnation. Under the somewhat misleading even though pleasantly alliterative title of *The Creeds of Christendom*, a living divine has brought together dogmatic utterances, Roman and Reformed, numerous enough to fill three massive volumes. The compilation has proved a most valuable help to the student; but when it is considered that the New Testament, the fountain-head of Christian doctrine, is commonly printed in one volume, and a small volume at that, it becomes evident that the makers of the Confessions have very considerably overdone their work. Yes, it must be frankly acknowledged that for no inconsiderable measure of the unpopularity of dogma the teachers of religion have been themselves to blame. They have tried to make men believe too much. Really it has been against the multiplicity of dogmas, rather than against the dogmatic principle itself, that opposition has kindled into flame. In order to form a just judgment in the matter we must learn carefully to distinguish between essential dogma, — those statements, that is to say, which make the essence of Christian belief, — and the many other propositions which from time to time have been set forth as logical inferences from these first-hand truths. When a living poet, in a stanza which has become hackneyed quite as much through misuse as through right use, speaks of our " little systems " having their day and ceasing to be, it is not, we may be very sure, the articles of the Creed he has in mind, but rather those complicated frame-works of theological opinion which under the name of platforms, confessions, and bodies of divinity have been again and again clamped and riveted together, only to fall in pieces as soon as there has been time enough for the corrosive influences of the atmosphere to eat away the bolts.

But the chief ground of complaint against Christian dogma is of another sort. I have been making allow-ance for what is justifiable in the unpopularity under which the word labors ; let us now look at what is unjustifiable in it. Men mislike Christian dogma be-cause of its unchangeableness, its fixity. The politi-cians have their dogmas, as we have seen ; but then they alter them to meet fresh emergencies, and re-make the platform as occasion may require. With the philosophers and the naturalists there is the same readiness to allow for revision. Our dogmas, say the metaphysicians, we are at any moment willing to throw into solution that they may crystallize afresh. And ours, chime in the naturalists, are only acknowl-edged stepping-stones to higher and larger and firmer ground ; we can, and if occasion arises, we shall re-vise them to-morrow. But the Church keeps on say-ing the same thing. She alone among the teaching voices to which man is asked to listen has nothing new to tell. Her dogma, like the Medo-Persian law, altereth not, and that is why we weary of it and wish it out of the way.

Here again the Church has a reason to give, and a sound one, as we shall see. Return to the Apostles' Creed, for a moment, and consider attentively of what sort of statements it is made up. In the very first clause of it we have no fewer than four dogmatic assertions: namely, that there is a God; that fatherliness is one of his characteristics; that infinite power is another; and furthermore that he puts this power into active exercise. "I believe in God the Father Almighty, Maker of Heaven and Earth." What is there here that the Church can fairly be called on to revise? If she had gathered these dogmas, as the political economist gathers his, by observation of what goes on in human society; if she had gathered them as the metaphysician gathers his, by observing what goes on in the mind of man; if she had gathered them as the naturalist gathers his, by observing what goes on in the world material, why then it would be perfectly proper to insist on frequently testing her methods and verifying her results.

But the Church maintains that she came into possession of her dogmas in another way altogether. She did not find them out; they were told to her. They are hers, not by right of discovery but by benefit of gift. The first paragraph of the Creed is the common property of the Jewish and the Christian

Churches, the second and the third owe their existence to the coming into the world of One who asserted Himself the Son of God; but all three sections
are alike in this, that their contents rest for authority
on testimony,—the testimony of men who have somehow made themselves believed.

But testimony once recorded must remain what it
is, unless indeed you can impeach the witnesses.
Here, for example, are certain definite statements
made by the first century writers as to what Jesus
said of Himself, of life, of death, of things present
and things to come. Out of them and other like
material the dogmas of the Church have been fashioned. We may reject the dogmas, we may utterly
refuse to receive them; but to ask the Church to alter
them merely in obedience to the popular demand for
change is most unreasonable. It is sometimes granted
us to forget what has been done, but never is it our
privilege to undo it.

> " Not Heaven itself upon the past hath power,
>   But what hath been, hath been."

The chemist may reinvestigate the atomic weight
of silver, the astronomer may recompute the elements
of a planet's period of revolution, but who shall call
back from the dead, John, Apostle and Evangelist, that
he may be cross-questioned and re-examined?

Has religion then nothing to learn from the new
pages man's finger is continually turning in the book
of knowledge? Has the Church no share in the

harvest of light in which the world of our time rejoices?

Most assuredly, Yes;—but the way in which the new knowledge is destined to help the Church is not by destroying her dogmas, it is rather by illustrating and enforcing them more powerfully than ever was possible before.

There is not an article of the Creed that has been shaken out of its place thus far by any thunderclap of discovery; neither is there one of them that has not been rendered more significant, more comprehensive, more august, by our knowledge of the things discovered. Holding fast, then, whatever has been with unanimity believed by Christians, let us read into it deeper and still deeper meanings, as knowledge grows "from more to more." The unpopularity of dogma is but a passing phase of feeling. The ages of faith have not really been outlived. Still, as of old, it is man's best privilege in regions where he cannot know, to trust; where he cannot prove, to hope.

Another way of reaching conclusions is by a study of alternatives. Let us try the *reductio ad absurdum*. Suppose that in a moment of disgust at dogmatism we determine once for all to throw the dogmatic principle overboard, how will it fare with us then? Very much, I fancy, as it might with an imperilled ship whose frightened crew, not content with casting the superabundant cargo into the sea, were to discharge the ballast also. Even when relieved of what threatened to sink it, a craft so circumstanced would still need something to steady it.

Nothing is more instructive in this regard than the experience of those who from time to time start out full of hope and full of courage to establish and to administer a purely undogmatic religion. Zeal for ethical as distinguished from theological interests is usually the mainspring of such movements. It is a most praiseworthy incentive; and whether the attempt take the title of " Free Religious Association " or " Society for Ethical Culture " or " University Hall Lectureship," we cannot but applaud the courage that refuses to despair of goodness even after the cause of theology has been given up for lost. But can an undogmatic religion achieve organization? Is it not like asking a jelly-fish to walk? The question is not intended as a slur, I put it seriously. The movement I am venturing thus incidentally to criticise is no outbreak of ignorant fanaticism; it enjoys the leadership of brilliant minds; it has eloquence and learning and moral earnestness enlisted in its support. What it is dreaming of is a Catholic Church of humanity, a fellowship into which Christian, Jew, and Moslem may enter unchallenged, provided only each confesses to an aspiration towards the true, the beautiful, and the good.

This new remedy proposed for our spiritual ills differs from what used to be called free-thinking in its attitude towards Christianity. Free-thinking was avowedly hostile to the received faith; free religion, to choose for convenience' sake one out of the many names the movement has taken on, disclaims hostility and mildly proposes conciliation.

Free-thinking was essentially destructive in its aims; free religion aspires, however hopelessly, to be constructive. Free-thinking placed its dependence on the head alone; free religion both recognizes and emphasizes the holy alliance between head and heart. Free-thinking had a baldness eminently repulsive to the imaginative mind; free religion exalts the imagination, and appeals as readily to the poetical as to the ratiocinative faculties of the soul. Your free-thinker was disposed to shut men up to hard-and-fast logic; your free-religionist is as ready as was Saint Ambrose to insist that not by dialectics only has it pleased God to save his heritage. In all this the free religion of to-day has an apparent advantage over the free-thinking of yesterday; it deals more fairly by the facts of human nature, it breathes a better flavor and seems to offer a richer promise. "These Christians meant well," it says, "but they have lamentably blundered. Listen, and let us make plain to you the secret of their failure." Any voice that utters itself after this fashion, especially if it be one that has in it the unmistakable quality honest conviction gives to voices, is sure of a certain measure of attention. No sensible person or careful observer is so completely satisfied with things as they are as not to be willing to acknowledge that they might conceivably be bettered. "You may be right," society says to each new prophet as he appears. " Speak out, tell us what you think. Propound your plan."

I suggest therefore that we look a little carefully into the case for free religion, as a preliminary step towards a better understanding of the dogmatic position taken up at Lambeth.

The initial point from which the anti-dogmatists make their start, is the existence in man of a religious instinct. This instinct, so the argument runs, is the universal heritage of the race. In greater or less force it exists and has existed everywhere, and in all. Climatic, temperamental, and other causes have conspired to give to the external manifestations of this instinct, which is still everywhere essentially the same, a singular diversity. Religions, like plants, have their classes and orders. One and the same kind of life pervades all forms of vegetation from the lichen to the cedar, and the scientific mind sees in the countless faiths of the world only the parti-colored clothing which the religious instinct of mankind has wrapped about itself.

It would be doing injustice to the advocates of the new religion to press this last illustration to extremities. " The meanest flower that blows " has as good a claim to a continued existence in the world's flora as any other. The Free Religionists would not say this of the meanest superstition. They would, to be sure, admit the representative of the superstition to their conclave ; but they would do it in the hope that the society of wiser and better souls would purge his ignorance. Hence they would give him, so to speak, a seat without a vote. They are not so weak as to maintain that all religions are equally true and equally good; only they would make their amnesty, at the outset, cover all, trusting to some happy law of natural selection to weed out error in " the process of the suns."

The illustration of the flora is, however, thus far good that it does explain, unless I unintentionally misconceive their theory, the notion of the advocates of the new scheme with regard to the origin of the existing state of things. Religions, so they argue, are what they are because the laws of the universe are what they are. We human creatures are no more to blame for not agreeing in one faith than the brute earth is to blame because she finds herself belted with zones of varying temperature, and districted among families of men who cannot understand each other's speech.

It is easy to see what place Christianity must hold in such a scheme. It is at best a *religio licita*, and only a *religio pro tempore licita* at that. Jesus may have his place in the new Pantheon, but the statue must stand upon no raised dais. The Nazarene must not overtop him of the Porch, or even him of the Garden. Indeed a disciple of the new religion will, if he be consistent, claim the right to sink Christianity a little below the level of average religions. A late leader of English thought plainly intimated that in his judgment the religion of the cross would be improved by a larger infusion of pagan virtue; and I well remember the adroit way in which a New England Brahmin years ago parried a question which some of his speculations had called forth. " Will not such reasoning," asked the disciple, " carry us back again into heathenism ? " " Say rather *forward* into heathenism," was the acute reply. Yes, let the Christian candidate for entrance into the fellowship of undogmatic religion fully and clearly understand that he goes as a contributor, nothing more. Whatever else may be allowed, the claim of the Son of Mary to universal kingship will never be. Our new prophets simply propose to cast into the blast-furnace of public opinion all the old worn-out creeds they can lay hands on, in the vague hope that when, after fusion, the molten stream of mingled faiths flows out, it may spontaneously run itself into some shape of beauty that shall entrance mankind. But the religion we have thus far professed has ever shown itself unfriendly to any amalgam or alloy. Christianity is at once the most inclusive and the most exclusive of all religions. It is inclusive, because it proposes to itself no less a task than the conversion of the world; but then the world is to be converted to Christianity, not to something else. Forget this, if you would enter into the spirit and the life of the new movement.

But why do I say " movement " ? If the new religion were only what I have thus far pictured it, would it deserve so dignified a name ? It might rank as a fresh system of theological eclecticism, but scarcely as "a movement" in any adequate sense of that word. And yet we shall see, as we look further into our subject, that in the very fact of its being a movement lies the really distinctive feature of the scheme we have stepped aside to study. For a number of metaphysical minds to interest themselves in following out certain processes of formal logic is one thing. For these same minds to attempt important changes in the structure of civil society, in order that it may the better harmonize with their conclusions, is quite another thing. Now this last is what the new religion proposes. To its recognition of the religious instinct in man, it superadds a recognition of the social instinct, and, rightly persuaded that no good results can follow unless these two instincts cordially conspire, it says, "We must have organization." But can there be organization with no formula of concord upon which to build? Can there be, I mean, any better and more lasting organization than is implied in getting together under one roof, choosing an officer to preside over the meeting, and appointing a secretary and a treasurer?

Not if it be true, as true I have been maintaining it to be, that all forms of associated life, whether secular or religious, whether called churches, states, confederations, fraternities, or leagues, owe their stability to a corner-stone of dogma.

The apostles of ethical culture have a great many beautiful and eloquent things to say about "work." We ought to forsake controversy, they tell us, and

take to working together in the fellowship of the
spirit to bless our fellow-men. Quite right. But
what is work? Waiving the very highest definition
of all, — "This is the work of God, that ye believe on
Him whom He hath sent," take instead some such
interpretation of the word as all will be willing to
accept. Here is one: — "Pure religion and undefiled
before God and the Father is this; to visit the fatherless and widows in their affliction." This is a kind
of "work" which all will agree ought to be done.
But how? Not simply by carrying supplies of food
and clothing to the house of sorrow. If there be
poverty under the roof it may be well, delicately, to
do this; but you are a sorry "worker" if you can do
no more. The fatherless and widows whom the author of our phrase had in mind were not necessarily paupers. What these orphaned and desolate
fellow-creatures of yours have the most need of, and
the best right to ask for, is the ministry of comfort.
You enter determined, in a thoroughly anti-dogmatic
spirit, to exercise it. You discover, perhaps a little
to your dismay, that grief has questions to ask, urgent
questions, questions that will not be put by. How do
you propose to set to "work" to satisfy this widowed
soul? "Tell me, thou minister of comfort," the
woman vehemently demands, "is there any hope?"
"Some have thought so," — you may answer, if you
will; but beware of letting any such tone of confidence betray itself in your voice as might offend your
brother the Agnostic, or your brother the Pantheist,

or your brother the Positivist. You are pledged to
"work" with them: "work" is the gracious object
that has brought you into one common fraternity;
possibly these brethren have happened to come with
you on this very errand of consolation. Remember
the terms of the compact. Your co-operation is to be
strictly "undogmatic," a working together in "the
fellowship of the spirit." Should you be rash enough
to tell those questioning souls anything definite about
a living God and a life to come, these companions of
yours would, as they valued truth, be bound to declare
after you had gone that your "living God" and your
"life to come" were only make-believe. Would not
the widow and the fatherless have been the happier
had they been left unvisited? Might not the doing
of such work as this more properly be called undoing?

This is not exaggeration; it is the simple testing of
a theory by the acid of common sense. If three men
cannot "work" together in comforting one household,
is anything better to be expected from those more
ambitious efforts that look towards the amelioration
of the life of whole communities? You may build a
benevolent institution as large as St. Peter's, and
write it all over with the catch-words of advanced
thought, but unless you have some better thing to say
to the unfortunates whom you put into it than merely,
"Be ye warmed and filled," it is a failure. The truth
is, this generation owes its aspirations after philan-
thropy to that very faith which it proposes to displace.
The first Napoleon has been called the matricide of

democracy.   The child of the Revolution, he scrupled
not to kill in cold blood the mother that bore him.
A ghost for ever haunts his dynasty.   Even so, should
our new religion become the matricide of the Church
of Christ, the memory of the sweet mother slain
would follow it reproachfully to the end.

Another fatal defect in the practical working of
the proposed scheme must lie in its utter want of any
cultus worthy to be called such.   By a cultus we understand that growth of usages, habits, observances,
and associations that springs up spontaneously around
any settled form of faith.   The cultus may be said to
clothe the dogma, just as the flesh of a human body
clothes the hard, strong framework upon which it
rests.

Public worship, consecrated buildings, sacramental rites, holy days and seasons, these make a part of
the Christian cultus.   But only think how it would
impoverish human life were all these things to be
obliterated.   What would become of art and literature,
to say nothing of social intercourse, if all that they
have drawn from the treasure-house of the Christian
Church were to be disowned and put out of sight ?
Look, for instance, at the only substitute the new
religion has to offer for the time-honored observance
of public worship.   A liturgy is out of the question, for
a liturgy must of necessity be inwrought with dogma.
Where there is uncertainty as to whether the God
addressed be personal or impersonal, all spoken
prayer is aimless ; it is impossible to give any pro-

longed utterance to blank aspiration; the list of the
interjections is brief. Take out of the Litany of the
Book of Common Prayer, for example, all that links
it to special circumstances, either in our Saviour's
life or in our own, and what is left? Nothing. The
new religion must, therefore, limit its public exercises
to an exchange of thought between mind and mind.
Lectures and discussions are its only "means of
grace;" a club, a library, or a reading-room its holiest
sanctuary. Should we be gainers by the change? I
venture to think not. Essays are entertaining and
instructive sometimes, and debates exciting; but are
these things valid substitutes for the worship of the
ages? Would they not be likely, in the long run, to
pall upon the taste even more seriously than the dull
sermons and formal prayers and lifeless hymns of
which we hear so much complaint? The non-Chris-
tian critics are continually falling out of patience with
our "cant." Does it never occur to them that, one
day, they may fall out of patience with their own?
No cant is so unspeakably wearisome as the cant of
unbelief. We can bear to be reminded once and twice
and thrice that we are in leading-strings, that we are
clogs upon the wheels of progress, that we love darkness rather than light, that the curse of barrenness is
upon all our thought; but really we hear so much of
this that one questions what will be left in the Millen-
nium of the new religion to form the staple of dis-
course. It is worth thinking of whether it will not be
well, even when the golden year of Liberalism has

come, to retain a few representatives of the old order for the purposes of practice in rhetorical invective if for nothing else?

But it is said, What need of any cultus? Let life itself, the common daily life of men, answer for the clothing of religion. When Sundays and Churches and Sacraments and all such ancient superstitions have been removed out of the way, then life itself will be so pure, so beautiful, that no special cultus will be needed to make it more so. Ah, we know what that means. We know what human life would be, robbed of all outward aids to holiness. We know that it would speedily become self-centred, grasping, churlish, sensual, devilish. Perhaps it is possible for a few men of refined sensibilities and a naturally quick moral instinct to cut themselves loose from the old moorings and still remain themselves generous, high-minded, and unselfish. But what is possible for an individual may not be possible for a community. We know that in England, for example, the refined Positivism of the Universities as it filters down through the strata of society thickens into secularism in the class just above the lowest, and hardens into animalism in the lowest class of all. And so we might find that were the creedless religion to be generally accepted here in America, it would cease to be, as it now is, eloquent in the praise of the Christian graces, and would become for the many the cloak of selfishness and vice. Listen to what Sainte-Beuve writes to M. Taine, — agnostics both of them.

"You make an observation upon my 'Port Royal.'
. . . There is a fine basis, you say, a broad basis in
natural morality, in virtue as understood by Aristotle,
Cicero, Marcus Aurelius, etc. I must confess to you
that what has always embarrassed the expression of
my thought in this direction and kept my adhesion
back, is the fact that I have not as optimistic an opinion of humanity as that which I see among all these
natural moralists. I am much more struck by the
miseries, the imperfections, the vices, the animal
coarseness, over which people imagine that it is easy
to triumph. This 'natural morality' of which I desire the reign, and which in antiquity was the lot of
an *élite*, seems to me very little advanced among the
moderns, especially if you consider the masses. The
nations which are praised *sur parole* and celebrated at
a distance, are found to be far in arrears. You must
be a Laboulaye before you believe that there is no
corruption in North America. Our Algeria is dy-
ing of absinthe; so are our manufacturing cities of
the north. If Rome is rotting, Geneva is becoming
coarse. I see everywhere an animality and a brutal-
ity, which discourage me and adjourn my hope of
the triumph of a healthy and scientific morality; I
am contented with admiring and respecting it in a
few."

This is honest certainly; and we have from a writer
of similar genius on the other side of the English
Channel a like testimony. "The history of self-sacri-
fice during the last eighteen hundred years," writes Mr.

Lecky, in the closing paragraphs of the book that first brought him into notice, " has been mainly the history of the action of Christianity on the world." He glories over the great advances of modern civilization, with which he credits the principle of free thought. " But then," he adds, " when we look back to the cheerful alacrity with which, in some former ages, men sacrificed all their material and intellectual interests to what they believed to be right, and when we realize the unclouded assurance that was their reward, it is impossible to deny that we have lost something in our progress."

Was there ever a better illustration than this scholium affords of Moses' boast, — " Their rock is not as our rock, even our enemies themselves being the judges " ?

The pursuit of undogmatic religion entails yet another disappointment. We have seen that without dogma there can be no concert of action between man and man and no cultus worthy of the name. These are losses that concern associated life. But it is further true that without dogma there can be for the individual no such thing as intellectual peace. Serious men are not content to catch at truth as children catch at fire-flies, pleased with success and almost equally content with failure. In the great emergencies of life, the mind brought face to face with the problem of destiny longs for the ability to say with a clear voice, " I believe." To man thus circumstanced the Christian Church exhibits her immemorial witness; while free religion offers him only the sorry comfort of a guess.

It is true that the " full assurance " secured by assent to the Church's witness is " the full assurance of faith," in contrast with the full assurance that follows upon demonstration, but the certitude attained is none the less satisfactory in the one case than in the other ; it avails for the purposes of living, and that is the main point. Christ's religion asserts that it has a distinct message for us ; undogmatic religion boasts that it has none, the broken chrysalis is its strongest argument for immortality, a song-bird its best proof that " God is love." The Christian Church meets a man with the Creed in her hands, the simple Creed of universal Christendom ; and she says, " I cannot force this faith upon you, I cannot compel you to accept it. I can only say that if you do welcome it, if you will make it the foundation-stone of all your religious thinking, there will follow, as consequence upon cause, intellectual peace. Of course there rests with you, in this matter, the power of contrary choice ; but on the whole, considering how this Creed of mine stands accredited by the past, considering all it has accomplished in the earth for peoples as well as for single souls, is it not a more reasonable thing on your part to believe than it would be to disbelieve ? Is not the case for faith indefinitely stronger than the case for no faith ? Does not the postulate justify itself in the results ? "

The promise held out by the adversaries of dogma

is an enticing one; "Liberty" and "Truth" are their favorite watchwords. But to be landed in negation is to find one's self fast bound in misery and iron, — a strange sort of liberty; and as for "truth," what is it worth to us if we are under oath never to set it forth without an interrogation mark attached? Augustine puts it well in the Confessions. He also, it appears, while philosophizing in the schools of Carthage, had heard this same illusive and elusive promise. "They cried out 'Truth! Truth!' and spake much thereof to me; yet it was not in them. O Truth! Truth! how inwardly did even then the marrow of my soul pant after thee, when they often and in many books echoed of thee to me, though it was an echo and no more!"

Passing now from the negative line of reasoning to the less ungracious and more congenial positive method, I call attention to a certain close intimacy that knits together two things, frequently, but most unwisely, represented as mutually antagonistic, "faith" and "the faith." Many persons now-a-days who confess themselves eager for more faith turn frigid at any mention of "the faith," as if an iceberg had suddenly swum into their sea. But the New Testament writers to a man are unconscious of the supposed dissonance. They never weary of ringing the changes on the possibilities of faith. Sometimes they seem to be thinking of it as an appetency, sometimes as an energy of the soul, now as the hand stretched out to grasp, and again as the mouth opened to receive; but, be it this or that, be it active effort or passive receptivity, faith as a spiritual characteristic stands at the head of the list, the one indispensable condition precedent to our knowledge of the God who made us.

On the other hand, we kill the climax of one of Paul's most animating utterances if we disallow the contrasted phrase, for he sums up the whole record of his life's struggle thus, — "I have kept the faith." Manifestly if he had kept the faith, there must have been in his judgment a faith to keep, — a certain something to be most surely believed, most tenaciously grasped, clung to through evil report and good. It is the tone not of one who has guessed out a philosophy of religion; rather he speaks as the man into whose custody there has been given a definite deposit of truth. Unless Paul in all this was utterly mistaken, it follows that faith has an intellectual as well as an emotional side, and that to define it as being wholly and only " a feeling " is a weak concession to the demands of the hour. The affections and the mind are both of them beholden to faith, and faith to them. In these days of easy divorce men clamor for a separation between head and heart; but woe be to him who puts asunder those whom God has joined together. "Faith" is the offspring of wedded heart and head, and " the faith " is the inheritance to which, by the terms both of the Old Testament and of its codicil the New, this child is heir.

Faith as an intellectual energy starts from the proposition "God is." Manifestly the mind must accept this modicum of fact before the feelings and the will can have anything to act upon. Whenever we see living flowers upon a stalk, somewhere we may be sure there either is or was a root. Dogma is the root of faith, and there can be no blossoming of the religious affections that does not consciously or unconsciously draw vitality through that. We risk nothing in thus conceding to the mind an important part in the act of faith. The vice of rationalism is not that it honors reason, but that it confounds faith with knowledge, and demands from God mathematical demonstrations of his truth. There is a difference between believing and knowing. Were there no difference we should not need the two words. I know that the whole is greater than any of its parts. I believe in the resurrection of the dead. Yet the believing is just as much an intellectual process as the knowing, and I cannot possibly say the Creed without an exercise of the mind.

But is this all? Have we exhausted the meaning of faith when we have found that it is the assent of the judgment, the acquiescence of the thinking part of us? Certainly not. Faith means more than this, a vast deal more, otherwise might the demons who believe no longer shudder. The biographer of Frederick Robertson tells us in one place how it was a characteristic of that sensitive and high-born spirit to be for ever pondering the question, What constitutes the essence of a "saving" faith? He rebelled, as well he might, against the notion that correct thinking could of itself carry a man into the kingdom of God. He was determined that his final definition of faith should, when he formed it, do full justice to the heart. And what does faith mean to the heart? Evidently trust, confidence, reliance, loyalty, — feelings all of them, and feelings moreover that call for a person, a conscious some one, towards whom they are to be exercised. A child clinging to his father's hand in a forest-path at night and feeling safe because it is his father's hand to which he clings, — this is faith. A woman believing in her lover's constancy although oceans divide him from her, and no message has come home for months, — this is faith. A boat's crew saved from a wreck trusting themselves wholly to the direction and control of one of their number, because they believe him most fit from his experience of seamanship to be their pilot, — this is faith. A handful of soldiers following a brave man on some forlorn hope, not forlorn for them because they love their leader and hold his courage as the pledge of victory, — this is faith. Heart-work in every instance, and heart-work moreover of a sort that necessitates a personal object. It is only by a metaphor, a figure of speech, that we can associate faith, the feeling, with an inanimate object. We may say that a workman has "confidence" in his tools, that a woodsman "trusts" the bough by which he swings himself across a mountain stream, that a capitalist "puts faith" in his bank; but in so speaking we use the words "confidence" and "trust" and "faith" in a figurative sense. These words convey their full and legitimate meaning only when it is a person in whom we confide or trust or put faith, for we can only feel towards one who is, or has been, himself capable of feeling.

This position once accepted, — namely, that faith means for the mind assent, for the heart trust, — it follows as a matter of course that there cannot be head-faith without a statement to be believed, or heart-faith without a person to be believed in. Faith as an appetite of the intellect demands for its food statements that are true. Faith as an appetite of the heart calls for a person worthy to be trusted. Truth and the true One, these taken together are what faith demands. How does the Christian religion set itself to the task of meeting and satisfying this twofold need? Not in any one-sided, scant, or partial way; not by freezing all religion into dogma, nor yet by melting it all into emotion. How then? Simply by so presenting what Paul proudly calls "the faith" that men shall see and own in it the living presence of the person Christ. It is told us in connection with Paul's visit to Athens, that the philosophers who met him in the market-place were moved to curiosity and willingness to hear him further, because he preached unto them "Jesus and the resurrection." Here in four words lies wrapt the secret after which many a weary seeker in our day has toiled in vain. Flouted by Stoics and pitied by Epicureans, Paul preached "Jesus and the resurrection." He slighted, that is to say, neither of the two claims of faith. To the mind he presented for acceptance a new truth, " the resurrection," to the heart a new object of affectionate confidence, " Jesus." Believe the fact, believe in the person, — this was his appeal.

Passing from Athens to Rome, what is it that we find distinguishing Christian people from other people in the days of the Cæsars? Clearly the holding of a distinctive and a definable faith, and the holding it with fervor. Whenever the populace raised the cry " The Christians to the lions!" there was always one way of escape, — renunciation of the faith. On one side lay the implements of torture ; on the other, home, friends, and a life of quietness. All hinged on the answer to the judge's question, Wilt thou or wilt thou not disown this faith? Evidently an undogmatic religion would in those days have saved many a life. But would the Church have lived?

> "If blessed Paul had staid in cot or learned shade,
>   With the priest's white attire, and the saints' tuneful choir,
>   Men had not gnashed their teeth, nor risen to slay,
>   But thou hadst been a heathen in thy day."

We do ill, therefore, to set " faith " and " the faith " in opposition, saying to the one, " Thy dominion is of the heart," and to the other, " Thine is of the head." A complete religion is one in which we see the faith spelt out in words that may be known and read of all men, while yet there is not one single letter in the whole epigraph that does not glow with flame.

The Bishops at Lambeth took up a definite position with respect to dogma. Their estimate of the measure of dogmatic agreement antecedently essential to the attainment of unity was expressed in the following words, " The Apostles' Creed as the Baptismal Symbol ; and the Nicene Creed as the sufficient statement of the Christian Faith."

When we remember how large an amount of dogma used to be insisted upon as necessary, this has, upon the face of it, the look of taking in sail under stress of weather, — and in that sense many observers, both within and without the pale of the Christian Church, have doubtless understood it. Here, they have said, is a plain concession to the menaces of criticism. Modern scholarship has proved itself too much for the confessions, and the creed-principle is evidently doomed. It is not to be yielded at once, but what we see is the beginning of the end.

Such inferences have a plausible look, and yet, when we think of it, all that the Bishops did was to reaffirm the doctrinal position of the early Church. Short confessions were the rule in the beginning ; to return to them is unquestionably an acknowledgment of having gained wisdom by experience, but is by no means tantamount to a surrender of first principles, — on the contrary, it is a solemn reassertion of first principles. Were the Creed to be reduced to a single proposition, that one statement would carry with it as effective an assertion of authority, as four-score sentences could do. The length of the armature is no test of the reality of the magnet. The question is, What is resident in the steel?

But over and above an implied insistence upon the principle of dogma, we note in the Lambeth statement an evident intention to discriminate between classes of believers. The Apostles' Creed is spoken of as a formulary for universal use; it is the "baptismal symbol," a thing to be written, as it were, on the very door-posts of the Church, an entrance lesson, a part of the initiative process itself. None is to be accounted too ignorant to be taught so much as this, none is to be thought of as so well-informed that with this he may dispense; it binds all: it is the minimum of Christian dogma. Equally evident is the intention to set forth the Nicene Creed as the maximum of the Church's doctrinal requirement, for this formulary is declared to be the "sufficient" statement of the Christian faith. In other words, the Apostles' Creed is to be regarded as the popular, and the Nicene Creed as the precise and, so to say, scientific setting forth of "those things which are most surely believed among us." It is not that the one Creed is supposed really to contain any more truth than the other, but only that the shorter of the two formularies is by its wording the better adapted to the needs of all sorts and conditions of men, while the longer more completely meets the requirements of those who critically demand of the Church her "statement." And I say this not forgetful of the fact that the difference between the two creeds finds its historical explanation

in the contrast between Eastern and Western methods
of religious thought. The Nicene formulary germi-
nated in Asiatic, the Apostles' in European soil, and
each reflects the intellectual habitudes of the region
that gave it birth. In other words, the distinction I
have drawn between a scientific and a popular mode
of statement seems not to have been had in view at
the outset. Oriental teachers simply expressed themselves after their fashion, occidental teachers after
theirs. But seeing that the two creeds do really, both
in form and substance, suggest to a western eye such
a contrast as I have described, the Bishops at Lambeth chose wisely in phrasing their utterance as they
did.

Turning to the question of the adaptability of these
ancient formularies to present-day needs, I observe
that the ultimate analysis resolves each of them into
the Christian Name of God. Whether we take the
Apostolic or the Nicene symbol, we find in either case
that the three paragraphs answer severally to "Father," "Son," and "Holy Ghost." In the one formulary the amplification is comparatively slight, in the
other comparatively full, but one and the same tri-
personal framework is common to them both. About
the name of the Father are grouped the thoughts
proper to creation, origin, and source ; about the
name of the Son, the characteristics of mediatorship ;
about the name of the Spirit, the unitive and energiz-
ing functions of the Eternal; but it is all one Name
set forth in one strong confession ; it is the voice of

the Holy Church throughout all the world acknowl-
edging the Father, of an infinite Majesty, the adorable, true, and only Son, also the Holy Ghost the
Comforter.

The special value of the Apostles' Creed for popular use and as a doctrinal test of fitness for admission
to Church privileges reveals itself in these four features, simplicity of language, brevity of compass,
positiveness of form, antiquity of origin. Because it
is simply worded, the unlettered can be taught it;
because it is short, little children can have it stamped
upon their memories for ever; because it is affirmative, it encourages hope; because it is ancient, it com-
mands confidence; that which has outlasted the
wear and tear of many generations will, we are en-
couraged to believe, manifest the same staying power till the end. It is true that "the new Astronomy"
(scarcely any longer new) and "the new Chemistry"
and "the new Biology" have suggested certain difficulties of interpretation in the case of two of the
articles of this Creed, the Descent into hell and the
Resurrection of the body, the stress of which was
hardly felt in former times; but the difficulties are
surface difficulties, and the putting them forward has
only served the purpose of making our insight into
the real meaning of the phrases themselves more
profound than was possible before.

The chief value of the longer Creed set forth at
Nicæa in A.D. 325 and given its final form at Con-
stantinople fifty-six years later, lies in its uncompro-

mising assertion of the divinity of Christ. This is a question that cannot be waived; it is the old test question " Whose Son is he ?" To treat it as a point of purely theological interest having no real contact with practical religion is to mislead. Between the two propositions, " Jesus Christ was a man, and a man only," " Jesus Christ was man and God," there is a great gulf fixed. Our whole attitude towards Jesus Christ is affected and determined according as we elect to throw in our lot with the one estimate or the other. If it be urged, as urged it often is, that while Christ was here in the flesh, the giving in of adhesion to Him was a much simpler affair, involving only an expression of personal confidence, the proper reply is that the essence of discipleship is now precisely what it was then, with this single point of difference, — that the present withdrawal of the Christ from the field of open vision necessitates our knowing Him by picture, instead of by person. The Creed is this picture. To wipe out of it the lines that indicate divinity would mean not merely to impair, but to destroy the likeness. Only occasionally, it is true, were even the twelve disciples privileged to see

> " . . . the God within Him light his face,"

and before only three out of these twelve was He transfigured ; and yet, just as we say of a portrait that it ought to show a man at his best, so may we say reverently of the Creed that unless it presents Christ to us at his highest it fails.

A criticism of a very different sort is sometimes passed upon the Nicene Creed. Theologians of a certain school insist that as a formulary it is inadequate to the needs of the modern Church, because it has almost nothing to say about "the plan of salvation," — lays so little stress on the natural depravity of man, and observes complete silence with respect to many of the points that seem essential for the strategy of present-day controversialists. But, as a profound religious thinker not so very many years ago remarked, "to base theology upon the dogma of sin, instead of on the dogma of God, is a mistake." Perhaps it was by their clear perception of this truth that the Bishops were moved to choose the adjective they did. "The Nicene Creed as the *sufficient* statement of the Christian Faith" is their phrase. "Sufficient" indeed it is, setting forth, as it so grandly does, what God has told us of Himself, and leaving unsaid what we may safely be trusted to find out for ourselves, in our wretchedness and poverty, namely, our sore need of the One who can be thus described. Yes, anthropology can be trusted to teach itself, for "what man knoweth the things of a man, save the spirit of man which is in him;" it is theology, the knowledge of the true God, we need to have instilled into us. Only let men become persuaded of the high dignity of Him who for them and for their salvation came down from heaven, and there will be little doubtfulness in their minds as to the gravity of the crisis, the soreness of the emergency, that made such a humiliation necessary. Among ourselves, the spectacle of another's greatness is often as effectual a lesson in modesty as painful meditations upon our own little-ness; and it is equally true in religion that when once convinced of the high lineage of Him whom the Nicene Creed declares to be one with the Father in whatever is essential to divinity, we cannot hesitate long as to the attitude it behooves us to take as suppliants before the throne. Was a person of this dignity "crucified dead, and buried"? The very statement carries with it an implication of unworthiness on man's part such as ten thousand penitential litanies would be insuffi-cient to express. That "the Infinite" and "the Ab-solute" of the philosophers is in reality such a one as the Father of our Lord Jesus Christ, such a one as the life pictured in the four Gospels would suggest,— this is what we need to be told, and this is what the Creed tells us. Having been told this, we may be trusted to give the right shading to our doctrine of human nature without help from formularies. When once the sun has risen, the eye has little trouble in picking out the dark spots in the landscape. We conclude, then, that in spite of its silence upon human nature and its depravity the Nicene Creed is a "suffi-cient statement of the Christian faith."

Doubtless even after this shall have been conceded there will remain for discussion and settlement sun-dry important questions of detail. Historical scholars will have to have their say as to the limits of the for-mulary; textual critics will wish to know all that can be known as to the authentic wording of it; while students of English are scarcely likely to rest satisfied with the present inadequate and, in some points, absolutely misleading translation. But these are fields of discussion upon which I do not propose to enter. Similar embarrassments have from the beginning beset all efforts to give currency to Holy Scripture, but in spite of them the Bible has become the great book of the people, and is certain to continue such.

The strong point of both the Apostles' and the Nicene Creeds as respects fitness for the task of unifying the believers is their sturdy realism. Modern creed-makers have condescended to argument; these ancient voices simply enunciate the facts. They set forth certain great objects of faith, and say to man, Look at them. They invite, not to the speculative discussion, but to the reverent contemplation of things that have been, are, and are yet for to come. The manger, the cross, the broken sepulchre, these after all are what make the real centre of unity. About these sacred places men of the most divergent ways of thinking may be well content to meet, suffering all their controversies to be swallowed up in the glad confession that "God has visited and redeemed his people."

The time for originating creeds, if indeed there ever was such a time, has gone by. You may make a brand-new one to-day, and fondly flatter yourself that you have put into it not only the accumulated wisdom of the past, but also all the newer truth that modern discovery has unveiled ; to-morrow's critic will find a flaw in your work, and before you are an old man yourself your creed will have been forgotten. Meanwhile, there will live on, while you live and after you have gone, those ancient formularies, incomparable for simplicity and sturdy strength, which have been the shelter of holy and humble men of heart through many generations, — "I believe in God the Father Almighty" their first words; "the life of the world to come" their last.

IV.

THE SIGNS AND SEALS.

All things, as many as pertain to offices and matters ecclesiastical, be full of divine significations and mysteries, and overflow with a celestial sweetness; if so be that a man be diligent in his study of them, and know how to draw honey from the rock, and oil from the hardest stone. . . . Wherefore I, William, by the alone tender mercy of God, Bishop of the Holy Church which is in Mende, will knock diligently at the door, if so be that the Key of David will open unto me; that the King may bring me in to his treasury and show unto me the heavenly pattern which was showed unto Moses in the mount. — DURANDUS. *Preface to the Rationale.*

Because there are two great sermons of the Gospel, which are the sum total and abbreviative of the whole word of God, the great messages of the Word incarnate, Christ was pleased to invest these two words with two sacraments, and assist those two sacraments, as He did the whole word of God, with the presence of his Spirit, that in them we might do more signally and solemnly what was in the ordinary ministrations done plainly and without extraordinary regards. — JEREMY TAYLOR.

IV.

THE SIGNS AND SEALS.

HAVING affirmed the relation of the Scriptures and of the Creeds to unity, the Bishops at Lambeth give the third place in their summary of essentials to " the Sacraments." Their *minimum* under this head is thus defined : —

" *The two Sacraments ordained by Christ himself, — Baptism and the Supper of the Lord, — ministered with unfailing use of Christ's words of institution, and of the elements ordained by Him.*"

Thus addressed, we find ourselves face to face with the great question of symbolism, — the origin of it, the uses of it, the measure of it.   In the whole territory of religious thought there is scarcely a patch of ground that has been more hotly contested.   Some go the length of making symbolism and religion contermin- ous.   Take away our tokens, they declare, and you extinguish our faith.   Others again are so nervously sensitive to the peril of conceding to the outward and visible sign the honors rightfully due only to the inward and invisible thing signified, that they let their dislike of symbolism carry them to the point of setting aside, as having been intended for merely temporary use, even the two sacraments ordained by

Christ Himself. Divergencies so grave as this are never without cause; the origin of them is usually to be sought far back in the very groundwork of human nature itself. But formidable though the task of search may look, we are bound to undertake it; for we shall find it impossible to do justice to the position taken up at Lambeth unless we can first attain to clear notions with respect to certain principles that underlie, not the two sacraments only, but equally whatsoever else there may be in life that deserves to be called sacramental. Undoubtedly the *nexus* that binds symbolism to religion is a knotted and tangled skein; but unless we can somehow contrive to straighten out the threads, we shall have to reconcile ourselves, as best we may, to a confused theology. To so disappointing a conclusion we ought not to let ourselves be shut up without effort.

By a symbol is commonly meant either an object or an action understood to be emblematic and representative of some spiritual, or, if not spiritual, at any rate invisible reality. Tersely defined, symbolism is that whereby the outward eye of the body aids the inner eye of the mind in the exercise of its own proper vision. I say this, not forgetful of the fact that forms of words are sometimes spoken of as symbols, and this too in direct connection with theology. A writer on dogmatics, when he treats of symbols and symbolism, has in mind creeds and the study of them; forms of faith, and not at all such forms as come under the definition I just now gave. Thus we read in Church history of

" the symbol of Nicæa," " the Athanasian symbol," " the symbolical books of the Reformation ; " and, in fact, this very summary we are studying has, as we have just seen, the expression, " the Apostles' Creed, as the baptismal *symbol*." This is clearly a very different use of language from that which we follow when we speak of incense as a symbol ; or of lights, vestments, bowings, crossings, and genuflexions as symbolic.

The reason why one and the same word should have two such apparently dissimilar meanings, is not far to seek ; and since it will involve no very prolonged excursus into the region of etymology, I shall ask you to go with me on the search.

" Symbol " comes from a familiar Greek verb, meaning to throw together. But one of the commonest motives for throwing things together is that they may be compared, and their points of likeness and of unlikeness brought to view. This is just what is accomplished by the material symbol. By aid of it the visible and the invisible, the thing seen and the thing unseen are thrown together, collated, so to speak, in order that by the aid of the more familiar the less familiar may be understood, as when we make *black* the symbol of sorrow, or *light* the symbol of truth, or *weeds* the symbol of the spreading power that seems to inhere in wickedness. This is plain enough ; but how came creeds ever to be known as symbols ? What is there about sharp-cut verbal statements of doctrine that entitles them to be given the same name by which we

describe a token or emblem ?   Why, indeed, unless it
be that words when we look at them long enough are
seen to be themselves nothing but emblems of the
unseen realities for which they stand ?   All language
is in its very nature figurative, representative ; and, in
the last analysis, is found to be a mere aggregation
of symbols.   This fact forces itself upon us in such
expressions as, "the head of the army" and "the
foot of the mountain."   It is less evident when we
speak of an action as "sublime," or of a man as
"ambitious ;" but a glance at the Latin lexicon
shows us that these phrases are in reality every
bit as figurative as the others.   The sentence "God
is a spirit" would seem to be, on the face of it, the
very negation of symbolism.   What could be further
from our notion of material things than "spirit,"
and yet —

> "The spirit doth but mean the breath."

Archbishop Trench, in his "Synonymes of the New
Testament," quotes approvingly Jerome's remark on
the Apocalypse: "There are in it as many sacraments as there are words."   But why not give to
Jerome's pithy statement a still wider application ?
Why limit it to the last book of the Bible ?   Why
not say of "Webster's Unabridged," *Quot verba, tot
sacramenta* ?   For it certainly is true of all words, without exception, that they are sacraments in the sense
of being emblems, — representative signs of the realities for which they stand ; the main difference between

them and other tokens being that in the one case it is
the eye, and in the other case the ear, that is addressed.
"Words," says Hobbes, "are wise men's counters,
. . . but they are the money of fools." The maxim is
harshly phrased, but it gives us the substance of the
whole matter in a nutshell, and abundantly justifies
the instinct that led the early Christians, with only a
dim consciousness perhaps of the reason why they did
so, to call their forms of sound words "symbols;" for
a creed, regarded as a summary or compendium of
"the words of eternal life," is notably a symbol of
God's thought.

So then, if we cared to enlarge our first definition
so as to make it cover both the dogmatic and the
ritual uses of the word we are studying, we might
affirm symbolism to be the conversion of the invisible
into terms of the visible, whether by the agency of
objects or of sounds.

Profoundly studied, the two sacraments ordained
by Christ himself are seen to combine both of these
characteristics of symbolism, — were intended, that is
to say, to help us both by eye and ear. They are
not dumb tokens, they are vocal; there are words
attached to each, and of these words the Lambeth
platform insists that they be unfailingly employed as
part and parcel of the actions to which they have
been by the voice of Christ authoritatively attached.
Both of the language of institution and of the elements
ordained, there is to be, so the Declaration runs, "unfailing use."

But while all this is true, we cannot help feeling that in the case of the sacraments, the material symbolism, as contrasted with the verbal, has the predominance and was meant to have it. They are never spoken of as doctrines, though they might very properly have been called that, were the lessons conveyed in the respective formulas of institution the only thing intended to be had in mind. In fact, they are rather actions accompanied by words, than words accompanied by actions ; neither word nor action, however, having value of its own save as related to the sacred reality to which the whole symbolism points.

We return, therefore, for the present to the study of material as distinguished from verbal symbolism, persuaded that here, rather than elsewhere, the clew to a just interpretation of the sacraments is to be sought.

We must remember that whatever else and more than signs the sacraments may be, signs, in the first instance and upon the face of things, they unquestionably are. No alarmist cry of " Zuinglianism ! " can put out of remembrance the fact that the Book of Common Prayer answers the question, " What meanest thou by this word ' Sacrament ' ? " as follows, " I mean an outward and visible sign."

As to what the outward and visible sign imports and conveys, that is a matter for further instruction; but that sacraments present themselves to our attention first of all as signs, cannot be gainsaid.

I remark, then, that material symbols or signs may best be classified, and most advantageously studied, as (*a*) commemorative, (*b*) representative, and (*c*) effectual. A commemorative symbol is one that serves to keep alive the memory of a past event. Medals and monuments are of this order. Sometimes there is an evident connection between the symbol and the fact commemorated, sometimes there is none. Medals usually tell their own story to the eye, but monuments have often to depend upon oral tradition to interpret them. There is nothing for example in the mere sight of the obelisk on Bunker Hill to suggest to the mind of a wholly ignorant person the fact that a battle was there fought. The pillar Jacob set up at Bethel, and the heap of stones he and Laban piled up and called Mizpah, were both of them commemorative symbols, the one of a vision, the other of a covenant. Joshua gave a like character to the twelve stones he caused to be laid on the bed of Jordan, when he said, "These stones shall be for a memorial."

As civilization advances and history begins to take the place of tradition, commemorative symbols, pure and simple, fall more or less into disuse. Medals are still struck and monuments built in connection with historical events, but nobody accounts our need of these things imperative, as it used to be accounted before the invention of printing. In cases where the ancients would have heaped up stones, we make a book and store it in a library. Still the liking for symbols solely commemorative is by no means extinct, as the countless memorial buildings and statues set up in our own country since the civil war abundantly testify.

What I have called a " representative " symbol is one that images, not a past event as the commemorative symbol does, but a present though invisible reality. The universe is full of symbolism of this sort, and human speech is, as I have already pointed out, largely if not entirely based upon it. Representative symbolism is, indeed, the very food and drink of imaginative souls ; poets cannot live without it, and philosophers and theologians are almost as closely dependent upon it as they. In fact, some have ventured to assert that the whole frame of nature, rightly apprehended, is only one vast scheme of representative symbolism, a delicately articulated and carefully enunciated Word of God to man. " Without a parable spake He not unto them." We may not be prepared to go all lengths with Swedenbörg, and to hold as he does that Nature is throughout, and in the minutest details, a counterpart and metaphor of things invisible ; still less may we be willing to accept his arbitrary and often grotesque interpretations; but no thoughtful student in any department of human knowledge can go far without discovering his dependence upon representative symbolism for the very tools with which he is to work.

Effectual symbols (the expression has an Anglican sanction) are those that not only represent outwardly either a past event or an invisible fact, but more than this are actually charged with power to bring about results. The commission of an army officer is a good illustration. The commission is really given at the moment when the appointing power, be it king or governor, has decided upon its man, but the " effectual symbol " of the commission is the signed and sealed piece of parchment or paper that empowers the appointee to act in his new capacity.

Again, the essence of marriage undoubtedly lies in the mutual consent of a man and a woman to be husband and wife. This is what constitutes the spiritual fact. Nevertheless society rightly refuses to recognize any marriage as lawful or genuine when the " effectual symbol " of some ceremony, either secular or religious, has been omitted. The invisible fact must consent to let itself be expressed by a tangible sign, ring, service, certificate, what you please, or it passes for no fact at all.

But while we distinguish between these three sorts of symbols, the commemorative, the representative, and the effectual, we must guard ourselves against supposing that the three are necessarily exclusive of one another. A symbol may be solely commemorative, or solely representative, or solely effectual ; but it is perfectly possible for any two of these characteristics, or, indeed, for all three of them, to be combined in a single act or object. A good instance of such a combination is afforded by our national flag, which exhibits the threefold symbolism in its completeness. The thirteen stripes of alternate white and red make the flag a commemorative symbol. They recall the historical and unchangeable fact that the Colonies from which the present States have grown were, at the time of the formation of the federal government, in number thirteen. But the usage which provides that with the accession of every fresh State a new star shall be added to those already emblazoned on the field, makes the flag a representative symbol as well, for the cluster is the emblem of the present fact that in the unity of the Republic as many commonwealths have place as there are stars displayed. Thus the flag is seen to be at once historically commemorative and politically repre-sentative. But more even than this ; for the flag becomes what we know as an effectual symbol when-ever it is employed for the purpose of asserting sove-reignty. When the stars and stripes were first hoisted in Alaska, the flag served as the effectual symbol of the transfer of that territory from Russian to Ameri-can jurisdiction. Can we wonder at the power of symbolism over the affections? Can we wonder that for a flag some "would even dare to die"? I have thus far intentionally drawn the most of my illus-trations from the field of secular life, with a view to making it plain that symbolism is not an affair of reli-gion only, but that it enters and re-enters continually upon the area of our daily interests and occupations.

Confining ourselves now to "effectual" symbols, with a view to the concentration of our thought upon the sacraments, we shall do well to make note of a certain diversity in the methods whereby the effectual symbols bring their effects to pass. A symbol may be of such a sort as to become effectual mainly through its didactic power as an object-lesson; or again through its control over the heart, either as a pledge of reassurance or as a means for the actual conveyance of blessing.

That symbolic actions and objects do have a didactic or educational value, and that their effect in this direction is a very real effect, Christian people nowadays are pretty generally agreed. It is in most communions simply a question of more or less, — the general principle is admitted. Time was when an open Bible, an oil lamp of antique pattern, and a few other emblems of the sort found in printers' sample books, made up all the symbolism the average Protestant would allow himself; but now, even the iconoclast, so soft have manners become, refuses to lay about him indiscriminately and holds his hammer at a poise before deciding to strike. Everybody knows what fierce battles were fought in Reformation times over the sign of the cross in baptism and the use of the ring in marriage. We must not say too hastily that these contests were idle. So long as the sign of the cross was looked upon by multitudes of ignorant people as a form of exorcism, and so long as the ring was supposed to carry a charm with it, opposition to these really innocent tokens was certainly not blameworthy, even though we may judge it to have been excessive. Men do right to resist strictly whatever they honestly believe to be the symbolism of falsehood.

As respects wealth of didactic power the two sacraments differ widely. The symbolism of Holy Baptism is exceedingly simple; the symbolism of Holy Communion exceedingly complex. In Baptism, the lustral feature is the main thing. The idea meant to be suggested to the eye by the "water wherein the person is baptized" is the cleansing of the soul. Our Lord in his discourses uses water as the emblem of that which alone can quench spiritual thirst; but such is clearly not the mystical or figurative value of this element as employed in baptism. Here its main purpose is to convey to the mind, through the agency of the sense of sight, a firm persuasion that as the body has been "washed with pure water" so the soul has in some sense, actual or hypothetical, we will not pause to argue which, similarly been made clean. "Ye were washed, ye were sanctified," writes Paul to his Corinthians, remonstrating with them for their lapse into the impurities from which the water of Baptism ought to have cut them off as by a Red Sea flood for ever.

When Baptism is administered by immersion, there comes in the secondary symbolism of burial. The man goes down into the grave of waters in order that, leaving there the dead tissues of a former self, he presently may rise again into the pureness, freshness, newness of the life called holy. But for the sanction twice given to it in the writings of St. Paul, this interpretation of the figurative significance of Baptism would probably strike us as far-fetched. It certainly cannot be said to commend itself to the mind of the observer as promptly as the other and more familiar translation of the sacramental action does.

Studied as an effectual symbol, Baptism is found to have for a chief end and aim the transfer of the person washed and cleansed from one environment to another. At least this would appear to be the teaching of Anglican theology, for, in answer to a question as to the inward and spiritual grace or blessing conveyed in this sacrament, the child is instructed in the Church Catechism to reply, " A death unto sin and a new birth unto righteousness." But the only thing that death and birth may be said to have in common is this, that each marks a transition from one stage or condition of existence to another. By natural birth man is brought into relations with society, he becomes a recognized member of the human race. Similarly by the new birth of Baptism he is brought into relations with all the baptized, and from having been simply a member of the race becomes also a member of the society of Christ. So again with death; that also as, Christians believe, is an event as contrasted with a condition; it is not an eternal sleep, it is the gateway from an old and inferior sort of life to a new and different one. In so far then as the grace of Baptism can properly be spoken of as a " death," we must be meant to understand that by it as by a door we pass from the worse environment to the better, from a state of existence clouded and clogged by "sin" into a state of existence made luminous and free by "righteousness." All this of course is uttered in the high and rarefied atmosphere of idealism. As a matter of fact, we do not always discern this edifying contrast between the lives of the baptized and the lives of the unbaptized, — would that we did! I am speaking of the theory of the thing. Possibly if we were to institute a like comparison between the theory of the State and the practice of the State, we should find an even more portentous gulf sundering things as they are from things as they ought to be. And yet both State and Church, be it never forgotten, are of God. We must not let ourselves despair of either of them. Of the whole body of the baptized we certainly may say with truthfulness, that as contrasted with the whole body of the unbaptized, it gives evidence of spiritual superiority. Armies have their poltroons and families their black sheep; but we do not for that reason condemn the institute of family life as a failure, or say of the army that as an instrument of conquest it is useless. The like figure thereunto, even Baptism, doth also now save society, for by it we are born children into the family of God, and by it we are enrolled soldiers in the army of his Christ.

I spoke of the symbolism of the second of the two sacraments as being more complicated, and for that reason more difficult of interpretation, than the symbolism of the first. Baptism, for instance, cannot be said to have any commemorative character, except, indeed, in so far as any usage whatsoever may be said to commemorate the originator of it; but in the case of Holy Communion the commemorative feature is, as we shall see, the most prominent; I do not say necessarily the most important, but certainly the most prominent of all. Baptism, again, is representatively symbolic in only two, or at most three senses. Holy Communion, on the other hand, possesses a representative symbolism so manifold that it is perhaps impossible for any analysis to do it complete justice.

I have always been impressed by the suggestiveness of that sentence in the Communion Office of the Book of Common Prayer in which we pray God that, by the merits and death of his Son Jesus Christ and through faith in his blood, we and all his whole Church may obtain remission of our sins, and all other benefits of his passion. - " All other benefits of his passion," — it is as if the soul of the worshipper despaired of ever being able thoroughly to search into all the wealth of meaning and of blessing stored up in that transcendent sacrifice. Remission of sin, — yes, that is one thing; but how much more, who knows? And so also with the sacrament designed to put that sacrifice as it were before our very eyes; is it not just what we ought to expect that the sign, like the thing signified, should be, with respect to its contents, unsearchable.

Nevertheless, even as we may without presumption or irreverence seek to look into the meaning and purport of the sacrifice itself, although assured beforehand that we can only know in part, so may we also with a certain holy fearlessness essay to interpret the symbolism prescribed by Christ himself as a help to our better appreciation of the sacrifice.

I pause here to observe that the controversy with the Church of Rome over the number of the sacraments is, in great measure, a mere quibble of words. Every theological student knows perfectly well that other things besides Baptism and the Lord's Supper passed among the primitive Christians under the general name of sacrament. The Latin fathers seem to have used the word in the sense of a sacred symbol or religious emblem of any sort. The Schoolmen, with their love of exact classification, gladly fastened the mystic number "seven" upon the sacraments, but had five or nine been needed by the Church authorities of their day, no doubt the metaphysics of Peter Lombard and Saint Thomas would have been equal to the emergency. Among the many conceivable sacraments, Anglican religion recognizes but two of which it is willing to say positively, first, that they were "ordained" by Christ Himself, and secondly, that they are "means of grace."

But to come back to our study of the Holy Communion. The first and, as I have said, the most obvious of the aspects of the eucharistic symbolism is the commemorative one. The Book of Common Prayer, the only authoritative mouthpiece of Anglican religion, insists upon this with doubled and redoubled emphasis. "Why," the child is asked in the

Catechism, "was the sacrament of the Lord's Supper ordained?" No question could be more direct, and the answer is not less so. "For the *continual remembrance* of the death of Christ, and of the benefits which we receive thereby." In the Exhortation of the Communion Office we have the same point urged, for we are there told that ".to the end that we should always remember" the exceeding great love of our Master and only Saviour, he instituted and ordained these holy mysteries. So then, whatever other and further estimates of this sacrament's significance we may be bound to form, it can never be right for us to neglect or obscure the memorial signification. Neither are we left in any uncertainty as to what that is which is commemorated. This frequently recurring act of reminder, this observance of which it has been predicted that it shall endure so long as man and the earth maintain their present relations to one another, is, in the language of St. Paul, a showing forth of the death of Christ. Such language suggests, even if it does not assert, that in that death there had lain some marvellous significance, some singular efficacy, something to justify the calling it, as we do when speaking devotionally and from the heart, a "precious" death. Nothing is easier than to explain away by surface reasoning the mystery of the great sacrifice. We may accustom ourselves to speak of Christ on the Cross in the same tone and manner in which we speak of More on the scaffold and Cranmer at the stake; but after we have, as we fancy, emptied the whole thing of mystery, flooded the entire field with the dry light of the reason, we look up and there, to our unfeigned surprise, stands the Cross still, as of old, riveting the gaze of the whole human family, in no slightest measure shaken or disturbed, but rooted to its ancient place, — the same easily explainable thing which yet will not be explained it always was.

The truth is, the essence of the Christian religion lies in the principle of sacrifice. There is nothing on earth so deep as sacrifice, nothing in heaven so high. It is the secret of true life, the witness of sincerity, the root and bond of love. We are constantly reminded of this in our purely human relations. Sacrifice whenever and wherever seen, if believed to be genuine, draws admiration. Look about over the circle of your acquaintance. Which are the lives that challenge your reverence, — those in which sacrifice is prominent, or those from which it has been sedulously banished? It is needful for man's spiritual well-being that his thoughts should be turned as often as possible in the direction of sacrifice. There is a call for some one perfect embodiment and illustration of the principle, and it is found in the person of Him who says in the hearing of us all, "Lo I come to do thy will, O God."

Sacrifice has never been wholly absent from religion. We trace the history of it as a formal rite from the earliest times. The smoke of altars rises all along the line of human history. A very dim and confused notion of the real meaning of what they did, those primitive worshippers may have had, yet must this truth with more or less of distinctness have reached them, that with the giving up of life in God's service there is associated the winning back of a better life. The man who came to the altar, and left there as an offering to God something that had cost him toil and effort, and went away with a sense of pardon and reconciliation, was still a long way off, we must confess, from the point reached by him who could say, "The sacrifices of God are a broken spirit;" but he was on the way to that point, he was being made ready to receive that higher truth. In the presence of the cross of Christ, high and lifted up, henceforth to be for ever recognized as the one authentic and supreme symbol of sacrifice, those old altar fires flicker and die. There is no longer any need of them; for now the Son of God is come, and in place of their dim adumbrations has given us vision to discern that the real sacrifice is a thing inward and of the will, only acceptable when patterned after his own. To keep always vivid before the eyes of the mind, and ever printed freshly on the remembrance, this truth that God's best revelation of Himself to man has been effected through sacrifice, this is what we may call the first intention of the sacrament of the body and blood of Christ. We do what we do in perpetual memory of the archetypal sacrifice. Had the fortunes of that great object-lesson we call the Cross been entrusted to tradition, the thing might have been forgotten, for records are perishable, and manuscripts may suffer mutilation; but the consecrated observance, the hallowed use lives on. Not only so, but even had the doctrine survived, what assurance have we that it might not have dropped out of men's regard, lost its hold on their affections, been distorted, cast aside as obsolete, caricatured out of all likeness to itself? Such a fate has befallen doctrines not a few; it might have befallen this one. But somehow as sacrament the thing endures, outrivalling tradition in persistency, excelling dogma in many-sidedness, — a perpetual witness to the love of Christ, an unfailing memorial of the tender mercy of our God.

An ancient name for the Lord's Supper is the Eucharist. The word has never fairly rooted itself in English speech, and does not seem to lose with time much of its foreign look. And yet it has a very simple and precious meaning; " Eucharist " is thanksgiving. Under what title could we better describe the true purport of a service from first to last so eloquent of gratitude.

But Holy Communion has other aspects besides its memorial and eucharistic ones. It ministers to that need of the soul which is best described under the similitude of hunger and thirst. Faintness and exhaustion are not confined to the body. The real self, of which the body is but the tent or cottage, that also has its season of weakness and insufficiency. The law of nourishment binds everything that lives, be it plant or soul. To possess vitality means, so far

as our human observation extends, to require food.
One feature, and it was a significant one, of the
ancient ritual of sacrifice was the feast upon the
victim. On what they slew they fed. They became,
as the phrase ran, " partakers of the altar." This
observance also Christ lifted up and glorified when,
in that upper room where He had gathered his disciples to eat the Passover with Him before He suffered, He turned the paschal meal into a parable of
the true spiritual nourishment. " Take, eat," said
He, " this is my body." " Drink ye all of this."
" This is my blood." When we have become familiar
enough with Nature's processes to understand how
it is that common food is turned to flesh and bone,
and these mortal bodies of ours continually renewed
and built up by nourishment, it will be time enough
to start minute inquiries as to those more subtile
methods by which He " in whom all spirits live "
repairs the waste and loss to which the soul is subject. Meantime devout and trusting hearts will continue to take comfort, as for many generations they
have been taking comfort, in such sentences as these :
" I am the bread of life." " He that cometh to Me
shall never hunger, and he that believeth on Me
shall never thirst." " I am the living bread which
came down from heaven." " If any man eat of this
bread he shall live for ever ; and the bread that I
will give is my flesh, which I will give for the life of
the world." It is not necessary that we should
thoroughly comprehend the methods of spiritual nutri-

tion whereby such promises as these are made good; it is a great happiness to believe that as a matter of fact they are made good, and that God does really feed the soul. True, we ought never to forget that the symbolism is representative, lest we fall into the error of confusing the material with the spiritual, so joining together things which God has put everlastingly asunder; but neither ought we to forget that the symbolism is effectual as well. The symbolism of parental love is effectual to the conveyance of blessing though we know not how. It is said that infants who struggle up into childhood without any fondling and caressing, most commonly show by unmistakable signs that the loss of what they ought to have enjoyed has told upon their constitutions. Bereft of all the pledges of love, the poor little things show like starvelings, even though they may have had as much material food and drink as other children. Disparage as vehemently as we may the value of outward and visible signs, here is an instance in which the lack of them has been well-nigh fatal to life itself. The truth is, there is such a thing as being too much on the alert against superstition. To believe that when the soul hungers Christ can feed it, that when the soul thirsts Christ can give it drink, — surely there is no superstition in this; nor do we superstitiously regard the symbolism of Communion when we take it to be effectual through the Spirit to this end. Christ is the real minister of the Sacrament. It is He Himself who gives Himself. The earthly priest breaks perishable bread; it is the heavenly Priest who says, "Eat, and thy soul shall live."

The real danger-line in eucharistic symbolism ought to be drawn at the point when a disposition to adore what is on the altar begins to betray itself, for here we do come in real peril of idolatry. With one consenting voice, the true prophets of God have from the beginning warned man against the notion that God can be worshipped under the form of any dead material whatever. The Roman doctrine of the Mass evades Isaiah's invective only by the forced conclusion that what is on the altar after consecration is not what the senses assert it to be, but "the veritable body of our Lord and his veritable blood, together with his soul and divinity." [1] Once persuaded that such is, indeed, the fact, the worshipper may with an untroubled conscience adore what is on the altar. To call such a one an idolater is slander. He is persuaded that Christ is there upon that spot as actually as when his sacred feet touched the temple pavement in Jerusalem; and, what is still more to the point, he is persuaded that nothing else is there. Why should he not bend all his worship towards the divine person so enthroned before his eyes?

The case is otherwise when we are invited to worship Christ under the "form" or "veil" of elements, which it is frankly acknowledged are what they look to be, namely God's " gifts and creatures of bread and

---

[1] Council of Trent, Sess. xiii., ch. 4.

11

wine." The appeal to the ritual worship of the Chosen People does not help the matter. It is true that the Old Testament abounds in material symbolism. The tabernacle and the temple were full of it. But of what were these material emblems symbolic?—that is the all-important point. Invariably they were symbolical of relations between persons, never of personality itself. The ark of the covenant, the altar of incense, the shew-bread and the lamps of fire, — these were all of them material things made serviceable for the instruction of the devout soul; but not one of them conveyed the suggestion of a Deity resident within or beneath the form. They were but tokens intended to reveal God's thought and his intention; they were in no sense the environment of his person. From the suggestion that gold or needle-work could in any way become the investiture of Jehovah, the pious Israelite would have recoiled as if one of Astarte's priests had touched him. In fact, it was their stout refusal to allow God to be worshipped by symbol that gave the Israelites the lonely pre-eminence they enjoyed. They were not more brave in war, not more skilled in the arts, not better versed in philosophy, than some of the other nations their contemporaries; but in their doctrine of God they stood alone.

The account given of the ark of the covenant, that sacred receptacle which in their sanctuary occupied the place of honor, brings out this point distinctly. Other religions than the Hebrew made use of arks. Sculptured representations of them may be seen upon

Egyptian monuments to-day. But what held they? An ibis possibly, or a handful of scarabs, nothing better; paltry images these of that divine Majesty which neither the heaven nor the heaven of heavens can contain. But listen to what the chronicler has to tell us of the true ark of God. The sentence I have in mind occurs in that magnificent chapter, the finest perhaps of all the spectacular passages of the Old Testament, the account of the dedication of the temple. Of this august scene the sacred ark, set down in what it was fondly hoped would prove its final resting-place, was centre. Stood there or lay there in it any material token, sign, or emblem of the adorable One? No; there was a symbol, but it was not that. The sacred thing there hidden was the expression not of the person, but of the will of the Almighty. "There was nothing in the ark," writes the historian with lofty simplicity, "save the two tables of stone, which Moses put there at Horeb when the Lord made a covenant with the children of Israel when they came out of the land of Egypt."

One chief provocative of the great revolt against mediæval notions of religion that passes under the name of the Reformation, was the desire on the part of the best minds to escape from such symbolism as was set forth by pyx and gong and monstrance, to the true and safe — safe, because true — position, that things spiritual can only spiritually be discerned.

Two other aspects of eucharistic symbolism remain to be noted, namely the two that are associated with the name "Communion." Even when the word is understood only of such intercourse as we hold with one another, we see easily how poor and tasteless a thing human life would be without communion. The greater part of such enjoyment as we have grows out of the interchange of thought and feeling that goes on between ourselves and those about us. Cut off from society, man sinks to something less than man. This is the reason why people are sometimes found declaring that they would rather be blind than deaf; a contention that looks at first sight insincere. And this is the reason also why, next to death, banishment has always been considered the capital punishment; even as excommunication was ever reckoned, in days when the Church dealt more freely in penalties than she now does, the extremest form of discipline; for excommunication is, after its kind, a banishment, being the shutting out of the offender from the communion, that is to say, the society of his fellow-believers, — the declaring him an exile from the commonwealth of God. We ought to think of Christ as coming in the power of the Spirit to meet us in this sacrament, as friend meets friend; not, indeed, as friends who meet on equal terms, but in such fellowship as Lord and liegeman have. There are those among our fellow-creatures of whom we say that merely to come into their presence is like receiving a benediction. We certainly cannot think less gratefully or less reverentially of his approach and nearness whose very raiment's edge carried healing in it for the touch

of faith. No doctrine of a real presence is so health-
ful or so helpful as that which seeks to draw us into
the real presence of the living Christ. If we go back
in thought to the night when the sacrament was instituted, and ask the disciples gathered about that board,
wherein their chief joy lies while they look and listen,
there cannot be any doubt as to how they will reply.
" We are happy," they will say to us, " because He is
near ; our comfort is in his presence, our joy comes
from his smile, our peace is in this holy communion
we are having with Him." This is what they would
say to us ; and what the real presence meant to them,
that it may best mean to us.[1] We have his own warrant for believing that it is the Spirit which really
brings to us the treasure of a more abundant life. It
is the Spirit that quickeneth ; the flesh (even were
their fable of transubstantiation true) could profit
nothing.

But besides this fellowship of the soul with the
Saviour, there lives in Holy Communion the further

[1] Compare the story of the walk to Emmaus, as told by St.
Luke. The obvious inference with respect to the nature of "the
real presence" drawn from the facts of the Last Supper is sometimes evaded by arguing that our Lord spoke in an anticipatory
way, and indicated what the elements were destined to be after his
decease at Jerusalem should have been accomplished. But at
Emmaus we see Him again taking bread, blessing and breaking it,
and giving to his disciples. When it is written that immediately
"their eyes were opened and they knew Him," can it possibly
mean that they "knew Him" as being in any sense resident in
the bread ? And this, be it carefully observed, happened *after* the
resurrection.

thought of a mutual fellowship among those who in one another's presence take and eat. How scantily this truth is realized, how feebly acted upon in everyday life, we know to our mortification. And yet even such a meagre embodiment of "the communion of saints" as we do have is better than nothing. We live by dreaming of golden times to come. We are for ever reaching after and hasting unto the vanishing horizon of our hopes. And of nothing is this more true than of Christ's doctrine of human brotherhood. It is spreading, slowly but surely spreading everywhere. Little by little the race is opening its eyes to the truth of the one family. Purblind visions abound; men are seen "as trees walking," and all that; but the eucharistic symbol of the one loaf is making itself understood, and onward, through dark and light, we move steadily to the end ordained.

Do we seem to have wandered a long way from Lambeth and the Bishops? It is an imaginary distance. At no moment since our first departure have they been beyond call; for dissent as vehemently as you may from all that I have been saying about the significance of sacraments, take a view as much higher or a view as much lower as you choose, our very differences will but illustrate the wisdom of these peace-makers, the Bishops, who insist that provided men will only use the sacraments; reverently careful, in the using, not to omit the words and elements ordained by Christ, they may, if they will, go on and philosophize about them to their hearts' content. Not so much by thoroughly understanding the sacraments as by gladly availing ourselves of them are we helped. The truth is, the sacraments are institutes not propositions. They cannot be explained in a hard and fast way; the manifoldness of their significance forbids it. It may be possible, and at times necessary, to say that they are *not* this or that, but to declare in set terms all that they actually are is far from easy. In this respect they differ no whit from other great institutes of human life. We speak of "the press," of "the ballot," of "the jury system;" but who will undertake to put into a single affirmative sentence all that any one of these imports? An institute is like a mountain or any other great object in Nature, you get the effect of it in a hundred different ways that utterly defy classification. I cannot say in a sentence what Niagara does for me, nor formulate in set phrase the impression made upon mind, heart and soul by a first look at the sea. Object-lessons differ in kind from language-lessons,—they are more intricate; they appeal to a greater variety of apprehensive powers within us; they do not address themselves exclusively to the logical faculty, but are on good terms with the imagination also, and take hold upon our lives, our hopes, our fears, in fact all that is within us. You can dissect dead systems of thought, you can run your knife edge between the two premises of a syllogism; but a living institute must be studied in its movements and its processes,

— at the too eager touch of a scalpel the life flies, and the secret of which you are in search goes with it. Try, for example, to analyze the process by which that holy institute the Christian home exerts its influence, — it cannot be done. All are agreed that a good home is an outward and visible sign of an inward and spiritual grace, but who will venture to declare precisely how and why it is such?

We have to content ourselves with saying to those who would break down the institute, — Destroy it not, for a blessing is in it. But how the blessing came to be there, and by what delicate processes of transmission it is conveyed, we cannot say in terms.

In a truly Catholic Church we shall have to reconcile ourselves to a very wide range of opinion with respect to the rationale of the sacraments. We cannot afford to purge out of our fellowship the great company of the mystics, those to whose hearts the eucharistic symbolism is as the very love language of the soul. We may not be able to think about Holy Communion precisely as they do, but that is no reason why we should not partake of it together. The man born without an ear for music does himself no credit, when out of his own ignorance he ridicules the ecstasies of those who are living in a loftier world than he knows anything about. Possibly there may be similar differences of susceptibility in the region of worship, and it is at least conceivable that to certain natures the truth of God and the love of God are brought home by sacramental symbolism with a power which, in their case at least, the symbolism of spoken words is unable to exert. On the other hand, let the mystical souls be themselves charitable towards the non-mystical. Let them remember that to the rigid enforcement of a "sacramental system," so called, the disruption of the former Christendom was in great measure due. It would be undoubtedly a hardship were poetry to be ruled out of life; but we are not for that reason to forget that prose is what makes the common medium of intercourse between man and man, and that it would be an injustice to insist upon the exclusive use of the more beautiful, and, if you will, more perfect form of speech.

The Bishops have therefore done wisely in setting the boundary pillars of sacramental usage wide apart. On the one hand, they make Baptism and the Lord's Supper an integral part of the Church's life, guarding thus against the constant drift of theology towards a philosophical idealism; while, on the other hand, they insist that, provided the words and elements by Christ ordained be strictly held to, we ought not to let ourselves be set asunder either by differences of opinion as to the *modus operandi* of the sacraments, or by differences of taste as to the ritual administration of them. Idolatrous misuse is by the very word "sacrament" ruled out on the right, a pseudo-spiritual disuse is ruled out on the left, — another way of saying that we are to use without abusing these great institutes of God, suspicious alike of the old alchemy by which the mediæval theologians sought to transmute the elements into something that they were not, and of the new chemistry which by a wholly different process would vaporize them into a metaphor.

V.

PILOTAGE.

It is a just and equal thing that every member of society should submit to the laws and orders of it; for every man is supposed upon those terms to enter into, and to abide in it ; every man is deemed to owe such obedience, in answer to his enjoyment of privileges, and partaking of advantages thereby. . . .

The same is also a comely and amiable thing, yielding much grace, procuring great honor to the Church, highly advancing and crediting religion. It is a goodly sight to behold things proceeding orderly; to see every person quietly resting in his post, or moving evenly in his rank; to observe superiors calmly leading, inferiors gladly following, and equals lovingly accompanying each other.   This is the Psalmist's *Ecce quam bonum!*

ISAAC BARROW.

The safety and preservation of the truth requires the ministerial office. As the laws of England would never be preserved without lawyers and judges, by the common people; so the Scriptures and the faith, sacraments and worship, could never have been brought to us as they are without a stated ministry, whose interest, office, and work it is continually to use them. — RICHARD BAXTER.

V.

PILOTAGE.

OVER and above chart, rudder, and compass, a ship requires the sort of personal supervision we call pilotage. The safe conveyance of the passengers is indeed the main point; but to this end officers and a crew are needed. Hence the prominence given in all consultations over the well-being of the Church to the question, How shall the ship be manned? We have already discussed the Scriptures, the Creeds, and the Sacraments, — possessions that correspond fairly well to the various helps to seamanship of which I just made mention; it remains to consider pilotage, or, as it is more commonly named, polity. Happily there exists no difference of opinion as to the actual headship; we all agree that Christ is in the ship; and where He is, there controversy as to precedence dies. It is a question as to how we may most acceptably and most efficiently co-operate with Him in working sails and oars; or, to go further back, it is a question as to whether He made provision, before his visible presence was withdrawn, for the maintenance of order and method in the execution of the task in hand.

Whether rightly or wrongly, the Bishops at Lambeth thought it plainly incumbent on them to put into what we may name their invitation an utterance upon this subject. The fourth and last of their proposed articles of peace reads thus : —

" *The Historic Episcopate, locally adapted in the methods of its administration to the varying needs of the nations and peoples called of God into the unity of his Church.*"

This opens the whole question of the Christian Ministry, — its origin, its transmission, its proper reach and scope. It is a large subject to be dealt with in a single lecture. I have no right to be ambitious of doing more than to let fly a few winged words of suggestion. Mere hints sometimes prove as efficacious towards the actual reaching of a result as labored proofs; at any rate, they are apt to be more kindly received by minds of the better order, for it is always pleasanter to be led to a conclusion than to be driven to one.

It is deserving of remark as a thing not a little singular that so few writers on the subject of the ministry should have seen fit, in handling their material, to begin at the beginning. Some start from things as they are, and finding in the Christian community of to-day a great and greatly diversified company of officials called variously priests, clergymen, and ministers, set themselves to constructing some theory of the facts that shall show this to be the best of all possible worlds ecclesiastical. Others go back to that period of Church history at which the ministry of the particular denomination to which they are personally attached came into existence, and are impatient of any doctrine upon the subject that would suggest or involve the need of earlier origins. Still others think, with a late Bampton lecturer, that if we would find the fountain of trustworthy information under this head, what remains of the literature of the sub-apostolic period is our true resort; though we no sooner reach this ground than we are met by a rival school, assuring us that we ought by no means to stop here, but to push on until we come within the actual circuit of New Testament times, and face to face with the apostolic men themselves.

But even this is not to begin at the beginning. I invite you to a line of search that runs back not only of the second century, but of the first. I suggest that we look for the initial impulse that finally brought to pass what we know as the Christian ministry in those words of the great Householder, " I will send my Son." Here we have an expression of purpose that antedates Bethlehem itself.

What I mean is that Jesus Christ is to be accounted the first Christian minister, not in rank only but in time, and that if we would understand what " the ministry " is in essence we must go straight to Him and study Him. Head of the race, He was content to call Himself our " minister," and laid the foundation of the " historic episcopate " by washing his disciples' feet. I am not at all scandalized as some

seem to be by the strong language of the Ignatian
Epistles with respect to the function and dignity
of the Bishop. Even if the words should turn out
to have been interpolated, a thing quite conceivable, notwithstanding the triumphant shouts of most
Anglican reviewers over Lightfoot's finished work,[1]
I should still be glad to accept them on their own
merits as testifying to a profound truth. To be sure
it startles one, for the moment, to be told that we ought
to think of the Bishop as representing Christ; but
if I were to change the phrase a little, and declare
that no Bishop deserved the high title of "Minister"
who misrepresented Christ, it would not seem an
over-statement.

The Christian ministry, — nay, I will put it more
strongly, — the Christian religion rests on the fact
that man is a creature who stands in continual need
of help. So plainly unequal is he to the task of self-
maintenance that he would long ago have perished
from the face of the earth but for aid rendered him
from without. I am speaking now of man in his
physical aspect, and as he finds himself besieged by
the forces of external nature. No animal compares
with man as respects the length of the period of
infancy. But even after he has been helped by
friendly hands over this long pathway of approach

---

[1] Ignatian Difficulties and Historic Doubts. A Letter to the
Very Reverend the Dean of Peterborough, by Robert C. Jenkins,
M. A., Hon. Curator of the Library of Lambeth Palace. London;
David Nutt, 1890.

to maturity, he would still have small chance for survival in the face of the tremendous odds against him, were it not for the assistance that comes to him through society. Single-handed, man would inevitably have succumbed long ago; he has kept his foothold by dint of co-operation, and co-operation is but another name for mutual help. What we know as the Christian religion is best apprehended when we conceive it as a divine provision for extending to man in his spiritual relations a help akin to that which in his temporal and wholly earthly affairs he so evidently needs. It is pre-eminently a device for seeking and saving what if unsought and unsaved would inevitably perish. Christ comes into the world as the great Helper. Quietly, through unobserved years, He makes himself useful with his hands; then He comes out into the clear light of public life and makes Himself useful by his words. "I am among you as he that serveth," is his motto from first to last, whether He speaks as carpenter's son or as Messiah. The very word we use to describe the three years, more or less, of his observable life tells the whole story; we name it his "Ministry." Christ then was what I have called Him, the first of Christian ministers, and the key-word to the innermost significance of his work is helpfulness.

We have next to note the fact that in actively carrying out this ministry of helpfulness, Jesus Christ made use not only of words but of persons. Himself the first of helpers, He must needs have those who should help Him in helping. "He appointed twelve," writes one of the evangelists, "that they might be with Him, and that He might send them forth to preach, and to have authority to cast out devils;" "whom also," adds another, "He named Apostles." Here, then, is a leading fact, full of significance. Jesus Christ appears among men and announces Himself the founder of a new social order, which He names the Kingdom of Heaven; and one of his very first acts, as legislator, is to appoint a "ministry." He gathers about Himself a definite number of men, invests them with definite privileges, and charges them with definite duties. We are not to suppose that these twelve men were the only ones in all Judea who were willing to leave their farms and nets and shops in order to be his companions. Neither are we to suppose that they were the only ones among the multitude of believers who possessed the requisite qualities for missionary work. Others may have been as devout, others as true-hearted, others as able; but He chose twelve, neither more nor less, and these alone He named Apostles, that is to say, messengers. It was not left to the chance impulse, no, not even to the serious inward conviction of any man, to commission himself a messenger: the appointment came in the first instance from the Head. "These are the men whom I accredit," He virtually said. We strike upon a principle here; we see that the Christian ministry bore at the first the character not so much of a task assumed, as of a duty assigned. The Twelve did not say to Jesus; "we have chosen you, and we will be your ministers;" but Jesus said to the Twelve, "I chose you, and appointed you." So obvious a fact as this would scarcely need to be stated, save for its bearing upon other matters to which we shall come by and by. That our Lord admitted twelve men to certain privileges, and laid upon them certain responsibilities which the great body of the believers did not share, must appear to everybody who accepts the Gospels as authentic, to be beyond controversy.

But was it Christ's purpose that this ministry should extend beyond the term of his own presence on the earth, or was it to lapse with his departure? Clearly the former of the two intentions was his; since we find these same men, after the Resurrection, re-commissioned by the voice that first appointed them to go out into the world in all directions in the capacity of witnesses, preachers and absolvers. It may be urged that it was only in their character of men who had personally companied with Christ, and could testify from memory to the fact of his Resurrection, that they were thus sent forth; and that for this reason they could have no successors, properly so-called, in the generation that followed upon their own. This objection certainly has weight, and does avail to break in some measure the force of what would otherwise be the unanswerable argument from the case of the election of Matthias to fill the vacant place of Judas; for we are expressly told that the election was narrowed to a choice from among those who had been personally known to the Lord Jesus, and had been eye-witnesses of his risen life. But when we pass to the Book of Acts, and to the unquestioned Epistles, and find, as we do find, an officered body of believers gradually coming into existence without break of continuity, we can scarcely refuse to acknowledge that, whether or not the apostolate was intended to last over under that name, a ministry that had the countenance of the Apostles, and, as we may say, held from them, did as a matter of fact emerge, and did as a matter of fact proceed to carry forward that very work of spiritual helpfulness which the Twelve were originally appointed to discharge. This is all I am concerned to insist upon for the present. We have for starting-ground, first, the fact that a ministry was by Christ Himself established to help Him in the work of helping others; and, secondly, the fact that a ministry answering to this one in all that was most essential, enjoyed general acceptance in the very first age of all,— namely, the generation covered by the New Testament writings themselves. Christianity, that is to say, set out upon its course equipped with a ministry as an integral part of its provision for the saving of the world. Man was to be helped in ways many and various; but notably, as in the day when Christ Himself was here, by chosen and commissioned men.

We have now to look with as close a scrutiny as possible into the nature of this ministry of help. The thing has scope and reach, method and manner, and these, to be appreciated, must come under analysis both quantitative and qualitative.

Of course that function of the ministry which at the first found exercise in bearing testimony from memory to the fact of the Resurrection, soon fell into abeyance. The body of men for whom it was possible in that sense to preach the Gospel of the Resurrection, died out. There were none left who could say, "I saw Him, spoke with Him, was blessed by Him after He rose from the dead." This is not to affirm that the place of the Resurrection, in the order of Christian preaching, has ceased to be a foremost place. Never since the beginning has there been a time when the duty of preaching Christ risen and living was more imperative upon his ministers than to-day. But what I mean is that in making up our estimate of characteristics vital to the very idea of the Christian ministry, and of necessity lastingly resident in it, this element of eye-witness is to be left out.

How and wherein may one who has never "seen Christ after the flesh," make full proof of his ministry, — fill out, that is to say, the circle which his helpfulness ought to cover? In seeking an answer to this question we might, if we chose, place our main reliance on the evidence of tradition. What men have always thought about the ministry and its work, that it will be safe for us to think. There is a good deal to be said for this method. The great callings of human life do retain their main characteristics through long stretches of time, and in spite of the changes that pass upon the world.   In matter of detail, in things accidental and incidental, there is alteration; but not in the proper work of the calling itself. Battles are fought with different weapons, according to changed tactics, cases are tried under new codes, diseases are treated by novel methods; but the soldier, the lawyer, the physician stand, in the main, in the same relation to modern society in which they stood to ancient. Their profiles are as distinctly outlined against the background of human life in general as ever they were.   So true is this felt to be, that we are not for a moment surprised when we find the dramatists of two thousand years ago putting into the mouths of their soldiers, lawyers, and physicians just such characteristic sayings as we are accustomed to hear from the men who follow these same callings to-day.

There is no reason why we should not look to find the like persistency of type in connection with the Christian ministry; in fact, we do find it.   Chaucer's parish priest draws our affections and holds our confidence as closely as if no great gulf of Reformation lay between him and us.   Nay, St. Paul himself, were he to come back to us to-morrow, and resume his interrupted work, would find it in all essential points just what he left it, notwithstanding the changes that have come over the complexion of society meantime.

But this appeal to tradition would hardly be in accord with the canon we laid down for ourselves at the outset, which was to keep as close as possible to the fount of ministerial authority, — Jesus Christ

Himself. When He used the memorable words, " As my Father hath sent Me, even so I send you," He gave us the golden key to the inner significance of every minister's work, and a standard by which to measure the completeness of it. For since we know from his own lips his functions as the eternal Minister to man, we cannot help inferring what it must mean for modern ministers properly to represent Him.

The Son of God has given us to understand that He holds to the human race three distinct relations, which, taken together, make up the whole of his ministry. He is our Prophet, our Priest, our King. As Prophet, He unfolds to us the truth ; as Priest, in our behalf He offers sacrifice ; as King, He rules us. All these functions of His He exercises in the world spiritual ; out of the darkness comes the voice that teaches us ; against a sky we cannot see rises the smoke of incense ; on supports no mortal hand has builded rests the throne. But these things are not unreal because invisible. This threefold work of Jesus Christ in men's behalf is as real as real can be, and it is for the purpose of making us the more sure of this that the ministry stands ordained. Those who receive it are charged as the representatives of Christ, his disciples, with a work closely correspond-ing in this feature of manifoldness with his work. The same law of triplicity that makes such a striking note of his mission is the note also of his represent-atives' mission. Answering to Christ's function of prophecy, stands the minister's function of preaching; answering to his priesthood, is the minister's leadership of worship; answering to his royalty, is the minister's responsibility for pastoral care. In what respect has lapse of time, the passing of many generations, altered or abridged this classification of ministerial duty? In no respect, save only in giving the modern Church a deeper and richer conception of what the preachership, the priesthood, and the pastorate should be.

Take the first of the three departments of ministerial duty, instruction in things spiritual, is it not in its essence just what it always was? Man has still to be persuaded to believe in God, still to be persuaded that this God in whom he believes so loved the world as to send into it his Son to suffer with and for us, still to be persuaded that fellowship with the Spirit of holiness is the only guarantee of peace of mind in this or in any world. These persuasions do not come by nature: men are not born with these convictions rooted in their minds; they have come, if come they have, through the aid of others, who as God's messengers have spoken to them, told them the truth. If these beliefs were really native to the soul, we should find them asserting themselves everywhere, without respect to race or climate, or the measure of civilization. They would be as rife in China and Japan as in America and Europe. In point of fact, we know that such is not the case. We know that these beliefs prevail in lands where the Christian pulpit has been set up,

where the voice of prophecy has made itself heard,
not elsewhere. Moreover, they are truths of which
the human heart and conscience have need. In that
sense it is true that they are native to us. They are
recognized, when once fairly seen, as being the very
food we require to keep our spirits from sinking
into death. But until they have been set before us
we do not see them; and the setting them before us
in such fashion that we shall know them to be what
they are and value them for what they are worth,
is the preacher's task. He does but take of the
things of Christ and show them to us, prophet in
his name.

Some are of opinion that this work of preachership
is coming to an end. Partly because the clergy
have ceased to be what they were once, the only
educated class, and partly because such wealth of
new knowledge is pouring into man's possession
that old faiths seem likely to be flooded and sub-
merged, the pulpit we are assured is doomed. The
conclusion is a rash one. As for the rise in the
general level of intelligence, so far from being a
discouragement to the preacher it ought to prove and
will prove his stimulus and spur. The preacher
differs from other teachers, in that his work is not
merely to instruct but to persuade. The truth he
has to convey requires a certain preparation of the
heart in the receiver, — the feelings must be touched,
the conscience wakened, the will moved, the whole
man roused into activity; and it is hard to see how

any increment of intelligence can free a community,
any more than it frees an individual man, from the
necessity of being brought under the personal influence of one who has been himself persuaded, if persuasion is to be made effectual. The teacher's chair
can never take the place of the preacher's pulpit.
How was it at the beginning? Andrew persuaded
finds his own brother Simon, and persuades him.
Philip persuaded finds Nathaniel, and persuades him.
Here lies the central power in preachership; it is
persuasion. How then can any access of intellect-
uality avail to make persuasion needless, or to su-
perannuate the preacher's work? Then as to this
promised inflow of new and unsuspected truth, this
enlarged knowledge of the universe and its laws,
why should that unsettle for a moment the foundations of the pulpit? Whatever goes to enrich the
common treasury of wisdom enriches at the same
time the teacher of religion. The discovery of new
truths puts no strain upon the Creed of Christendom;
that Creed is not a brittle thing that it should break.
What happens to the Creed when larger knowledge
comes to man, is simply what happened to it in your
mind and mine when we passed from childhood into
maturity, — it takes on a grander meaning, is interpreted by a more worthy standard, in a word, is better
appreciated than before. Christianity is the religion
of light. It has everything to hope and nothing to
fear from more light. Time may irradiate the Creed,
it never will annul it.

To the prophetic or teaching office the minister as reflecting or representing Christ adds intercession, priesthood. He is the recognized leader of his people's worship. Here again we come upon the question of transitoriness or permanency. Is worship on the decline? Are men ceasing to care to pray? Has the altar become a meaningless symbol? and will the voice of supplication presently be hushed through all the world? Some are faint hearted enough to think so. But philosophy and history, let alone theology, ought to make us ashamed of entertaining such a fear. Man is a worshipping creature. The book of his biography is full of the proofs of this. As well forbid the smoke to rise, as forbid the heart to pray. The great needs of the soul are permanent, — forgiveness, quietness of mind, courage to bear the ills of life, comfort in bereavement, guidance amid the difficulties of the way, — can we imagine a state of civilization, no matter how far advanced, in which man will cease to feel a hungering desire for these? No student of liturgics can fail to be impressed by the marvellous vitality of certain ancient prayers. Most of them were originally put into words by men who lived and died more than a thousand years ago. Within that period many growths have had time to spring up and to pass away, empires have risen, flourished, and decayed, but these simple forms of supplication have not become antiquated; no man wearies of the Collect for Peace, and the Collect for Grace; no one desires any new

thing in their stead. They are as fresh as they were
when they fell from the lips of the men who made
them. The very reason why they were treasured up,
accepted as the family jewels of the household of God,
was their indestructibility. Men saw that they had
in them that which could not die, and time has
justified the judgment. No doubt priesthood like
prophecy must adapt itself in some measure to the
circumstances of season and place. The temper of
one generation may be more friendly or more hostile
than was the temper of its predecessor to simplicity
and plainness in the forms of worship. One race
may take more kindly than another to ritual and
ceremonial. But these considerations are foreign to
the main point, which is, that the instinct of worship, the disposition to look up, the desire to plead
with the mysterious power that holds the keys of
life and of death, is in us as a part of ourselves,
not to be criticised as if it were a passing fashion,
not to be ridiculed out of existence or bargained
with to come to an end and cease. Priesthood, then,
like prophecy is permanent so long as the age endures. What shall happen to them after that hidden day when "cometh the end" none can tell; but
while the world continues, and seed-time and harvest,
summer and winter, day and night, are what they
are, the pulpit and the altar will hold their places.

But what now of the third great office of the one
Mediator, the kingship? Is there anything answering to that in the work of the Christian ministry?

At first we are disposed to cry, " Certainly there is not, and cannot be. We are the citizens of a Republic. There must be no ingredient of royalty in any ministry that attempts to minister to us." And yet if the main thought which has underlain all that I have been saying be a true thought, if the ministry of man to his fellow-man be indeed meant to shadow forth and represent the work of Christ Himself, it must be that there is something in this sacred office answering to the kingship of the Lord. You will, I am sure, acquit the suggestion of any taint of arrogance or pride when I define that answering something as being, what it is, the minister's pastoral duty. It is hard to associate absolutism, or any of the offensive features of royalty, with so simple, so inoffensive a symbol as the shepherd's crook. And yet the best and purest tradition of royalty after all is that which identifies the sceptre with the pastoral staff. The Homeric monarch is the shepherd of the people. No fault can be found with a kingship which glories in making itself useful. What more Christlike in the line of conduct has been seen in these times than the spectacle of the man whose style declares him " by the grace of God and by the will of the people, King of Italy," going deliberately into the city of the plague, determined there to remain allaying panic by his presence until the pestilence should be stayed. The sceptre of such a monarch is transfigured into the pastoral staff, and men see in him a fulfilment of the gracious words, " the good Shepherd giveth his life for the sheep." Will any one care to deny to the minister of Christ this royal prerogative of service?

Our own times have witnessed very considerable modifications in the department of pastoral care, — in large cities especially the change has been most noticeable. There is about it vastly more of what must be called, though with no disparaging intent, machinery. We classify and specialize in the work of doing good to a degree never known before, and what used to be regarded as the simple task of caring for the flock has become so complicated a thing, that administrative gifts and executive ability have acquired a market value, and are accounted almost as essential in the Christian minister as goodness of heart. And yet, after all, it is goodness of heart that must lie behind all the activity and animate all the mechanism, or presently we find the rattle of the wheels and shafts drowning the music of our worship. As with the prophetic and the priestly sides of the minister's work, so with the pastoral side; the pith, the heart of the thing has been the same from the beginning, in spite of shifting forms and changing methods and new names. The essence of pastoral duty is sympathy; in the eye of the true shepherd his own flock is always his "beautiful flock." To care for the needy in his distress, to comfort the sorrowful, to cheer the desponding heart, to win back the wandering, to seek the lost, and to do this for the love of it, — such is true pastoral success, such the kind of service that best reflects the royalty of Christ.

The question next presents itself, — and a deeply interesting question it is, — Did Christ intend this Ministry of his to abide in the world as an institute or as a succession; which? By an institute I mean a form or mode of life which has permanency for one of its main characteristics, but which is not so absolutely dependent upon a continuous existence that it can by no means be reproduced or reconstructed if once broken up. Take monarchy, than which there could not be a better illustration of my thought. We speak of the institute of monarchy, meaning by the phrase that method of civil government which accords supreme authority to one person who is theoretically irremovable. It is of the utmost importance to the prestige of monarchy that there should be associated with it the legend of a long past during which power has been handed on from ruler to ruler without break. Legitimacy is another thought that consorts easily and pleasantly with monarchy. Kings have always felt themselves strengthened, and, in point of fact, have been greatly reinforced by the prevalence of a popular belief in their divine right to rule. As the anointed of the Lord, a king may do and dare many things which subjects sceptical of his being such, would not tolerate. And yet monarchy pure and simple, monarchy the institute, is really independent of both of these adjuncts of antiquity and legitimacy; it can be established where it has never existed, and it can be restored in lands where after having once flourished it was overthrown and put away. We speak of the English monarchy as having lasted a thousand years; but this does not mean that during that long period there has been a continuous and unbroken line of kings and queens whose titles to the crown were flawless. It is the institute of monarchy that has endured; the principle of legitimacy has suffered violence more than once. Again, we have distinctions between different kinds of monarchy: there is absolute monarchy, limited monarchy, hereditary monarchy, elective monarchy; — these are all of them varieties of the one institute, the only essential requirement of which is that the social system shall be pyramidal, with one man at the top.

Very unlike what I have called the institute is the body known in law as the close corporation. Here the element of succession is paramount. A close corporation is made up of members empowered to fill the vacancies in their own number as they arise, and who are thus enabled to secure for the organism of which they are parts, a kind of earthly immortality. But if, by any chance, death does befall the corporation, there is then an utter end. The institute, as we saw, may be revived, restored, reestablished; but the close corporation once dead is dead for ever. This is the penalty it pays for resembling so nearly as it does, in assimilative and reparative power, the human body, and for enjoying a sort of personal identity to which the institute lays no claim. Under one or other of these two heads, most of the existing opinions about the nature of the ministry may be marshalled. Men incline to think of the thing either as admitting of revival and reconstruction when occasion calls, or else as a succession to which the characteristic of unbroken continuity is all essential. Which of the two theories is right, and which is wrong? With some diffidence I venture to suggest that neither view is defensible unless account be also taken of the other. Before hastily stigmatizing this line of remark as unworthy, it may be well to consider what there is to be said in behalf of each of the two sides. It will facilitate the discussion to call the one conception of the nature of the ministry the institutional, and the other the successional idea.

In favor of the institutional idea may be pleaded, first of all, the analogy of civil government, which is itself plainly an institute rather than a succession. The notion of a "social contract," as an historical event of the remote past, in virtue of which man came under government, has indeed been laughed out of court; but that it is possible for men to band together, originate courts of justice, choose rulers, and set up a state wholly out of continuity with any previously existing authority, is too plain to need demonstration. What is known in diplomacy as the recognition of a new sovereignty — an act of frequent occurrence — is evidence in point. But if the civil

society may, under the stress of necessity, or of what
looks like necessity, make to itself rulers and guides
who stand in no direct successional relation to any
antecedent authorities, why may not the spiritual
society do the same? If a company of explorers,
adventurers, if you will, have the right, in entering
upon possession of some newly discovered and wholly
unoccupied territory in Central Africa, to set up a
civil order in virtue of their manhood, and of the
social bond that necessarily exists where two or three
are gathered together, why may they not also set up a
holy order, and call upon it to minister the word and
sacraments? "Authority" is a subtle word not easy
to define; but whatever it may mean, it is difficult to
see how anybody who believes both Church and State
to have come from God can deny under the one form
of social order what he concedes under the other; can
admit, that is to say, the possible origination of a king,
while refusing to admit the possible origination of a
priest. Not to revive the somewhat stale illustration
of the desert island and the Bible washed ashore, let
us suppose every minister of the Christian religion, of
whatever name, the world over, were to be struck dead
to-night, would not the spiritual society, in virtue of
the powers lodged in it by the Head, be able to
reproduce the institute of the Ministry? Hooker,
than whom the science of Polity owns no greater
master, evidently was of opinion that this question
should be answered in the affirmative. This is what
he says: —

" Another extraordinary kind of vocation is, when the exigence of necessity doth constrain to leave the usual ways of the Church, which otherwise we would willingly keep ; where the Church must needs have some ordained and neither hath nor can have possibly a bishop to ordain ; in case of such necessity, the ordinary institution of God hath given oftentimes, and may give, place. And therefore we are not simply without exception to urge a lineal descent of power from the Apostles by continued succession of bishops in every effectual ordination." [1]

Again, there is the very powerful argument derivable from observation of results. If a piece of steel is shown me, I do not deny it to be steel merely because I happen to know that it was made by the Bessemer process. That process was for some time looked at suspiciously as an innovation ; but it held its ground, and secured establishment and recognition, and for the sufficient reason that the steel made in accordance with its formula was found to be good steel. It is not to be wondered at that men should reason after a like fashion with respect to the ministry and the products of the ministry. The proper product of the ministry is character. Bishops, priests, and deacons exist primarily in order that souls may through their instrumentality be rounded into symmetry, — made what God meant them to be. Any ecclesiastical philosophizing that tends to blur this great central fact of all, is self-condemned. The Church is God's device

---

[1] Eccles. Polity, Book VII. xiv. [11].

for bringing spiritual fruit to perfection. If ever the under-gardeners forget this, and from fear of "the wild boar out of the wood" turn all their attention to keeping the hedges in repair, the purpose of the Householder is thwarted.

When, therefore, we see, as we cannot help seeing unless our eyes are wilfully and persistently shut, that unique product known as Christian character abundantly developed under a ministry of the word and sacraments that does not claim for itself successional validity, we are moved to cry, What does it matter whether Holy Orders have the sort of legitimacy conferred by unbroken continuity of transmission or not?—here is the thing itself to produce which Holy Orders were originally designed; let us reason back from the fruit to the tree, from the cluster to the vine; if the thing borne is good, it must be that the stock from which it sprang is healthy. Moreover, this position appears to be strongly buttressed by a most suggestive precedent in Christ's own ministry. I mean, of course, the case of the man whom even the beloved Apostle desired to see formally condemned, because, while following not with the Twelve, he yet ventured upon casting out devils in the holy Name. The parallelism here would seem to be perfect; and is, in fact, so singularly striking, that for those who believe the Gospels to have been written for our learning, it must be hard not to see in it an intended lesson for us of these denominational days. The man was in the strictest sense of the word a volunteer. He had received no commission, not even the most informal one. But he had, so to say, all alone by himself, fallen in love with Jesus Christ; and finding himself, like Stephen, full of faith and of the Holy Ghost, had assumed to exercise that primary function of the ministry of help, — the driving out of those evil tenants that bar the gate of the soul against God's entrance.

Very possibly some of the Apostles, with the story of Dathan and Abiram fresh in mind, had looked to see the earth open and swallow him up; failing this, the least they could expect was that his mouth should be officially shut, and his exorcisms declared invalid. But no, nothing of the sort ensued; Christ was content simply to utter that weighty sentence, which ought to be named the golden rule of ecclesiastical polity, — "Forbid him not, for there is no man which shall do a miracle in my name that can lightly speak evil of me. For he that is not against us is on our part." It is true that we have in another connection the contrasted saying, "He that is not for me is against me;" but there is no real conflict of purport in the two dicta. In declaring that whoever is not for Him is against Him, Christ speaks in the singular number, and what He has in mind is the necessity of whole-heartedness in religion. Personal loyalty, He is reminding us, admits of no compromises. "No man can serve two masters" is his other way of putting the same thought. But in his comment on the doings of the self-appointed minister

whom the duly authorized Apostles desired to see put
out of countenance, our Lord uses not the singular
but the plural. The word is not " me " but " us,"
and for the simple reason that in this case the question of personal allegiance is not raised at all. It is
not so much as alleged that the man is casting out
devils boastfully in his own name; he is confessedly
doing it in Christ's name. But if so he must be
personally on Christ's side, and wholly on Christ's
side. He would be powerless to cast out devils if he
were not. The only trouble with him is that he has
failed to discern, and to identify himself with, the
true " stream of tendency." And yet, in spite of this,
what he does is not thrown away; the little tribu-
tary rills that flow with but slight momentum into
the river as it moves strongly on, may not seem to
add very much either to the volume or to the swift-
ness of the current; but in so far as they are " not
against " it, they may fairly enough be said to be
" for " it. The river could flow without any particular one of them; but they all help. Not to any
voluntary association for the promotion of Christianity does the promise run that the gates of hell shall
not prevail against it, and yet there is nothing to
forbid that the rivers of the flood thereof should
make glad the city of God. Surely this is a better
way of estimating modern denominationalism in its
relation to Christendom as a whole, than to go rum-
maging about among the early centuries, bent on discovering the particular heresies and sects to which

present-day forms of Christianity may with most of likelihood be compared.

And this gives me an easy point of transition to the other side of the argument, for the argument, as I began by insisting, has its two sides. Although Christ was full of charity for the volunteer exorcist, and flatly refused either to censure or to silence him, He showed by the very language He employed that He considered the advantage to lie with the main body, — with those who were serving under a system of orderly appointment. What other meaning can we attach to those phrases, " with us," " on our side "? Who are included in these plurals? Clearly and beyond all question the Apostles themselves. There is a side; God's battle has begun; and the Leader says to his staff, Don't quarrel with anybody whom you find fighting in my name, even if he be nothing more than a skirmisher; he is on our side.

Let us look then at some of the strong points of the successional idea. The great advantage of strict notions with respect to the orderly handing on of authority is that they make for the interest of reverence and tranquillity. Grant that there may be times when it is needful to shock reverence and to break up tranquillity, concede in other words the abstract " right of revolution " for cause; nevertheless, it will hardly be disputed that alike in State and Church reverence and tranquillity are desirable possessions where they may be had. Hence even democracies are careful not to dispense wholly with the visible and audible welding process whereby the incoming administration is fastened to the outgoing one. No appearance of absolute fracture is permitted; the government is, as we say, handed on. This conserves reverence for authority, and helps the maintenance of quietness; for legitimacy takes sanction from the past, and even Republics grow stronger after they have had time to age. The mere fact of our knowing that not a civil government on earth can boast of having held its authority in unbroken continuity from time immemorial, does not nullify this sort of reverence in us. True, we say to ourselves, there is but one river of authority that flows on endlessly; all power is of God; but it is well to approximate as nearly as we can to the stately movement of that eternal stream. We will not needlessly and wantonly break with the past. Hence we have in ecclesiastical history the noteworthy fact, that spiritual communities to whom what I have called the successional idea is bitterly repugnant because they cannot without torturing the record reconcile it with their actual beginnings, are often markedly tenacious of whatever prestige may have come to the body denominational by dint of long survival and continuance. They feel that a slur is cast upon their ministry if it be ranked with that of a sect born yesterday. But if there be nothing at all in the successional idea, if the whole notion of transmitted holy orders be delusive, anti-democratic, and unspiritual, why should there be, under the supposed circumstances, any such pride of place, any disposition to look patronizingly on the latest born in the denominational family? Ought it not rather, in its rôle of infant Church, to be welcomed and to have everything made pleasant for it? It would appear, therefore, that even those who repudiate in terms the successional principle, do tacitly attach a certain amount of importance to it. They are unwilling to base their ministry upon that idea; but neither do they object to seeing that idea become historically associated with their ministry. Other things being equal, they hold it desirable that authority should be transmitted in an orderly and peaceable manner, although if it were necessary to fight for the institutional as against the successional conception of the nature of the ministry, fight they would.

Broadly speaking, we may say that one of these two ways of looking at the thing is characteristic of the Catholic; the other, of the Protestant mind. All Romanists, most Anglicans, many Presbyterians, make much of the successional aspect of the ministry. With more or less of insistence they demand of any one who proposes to exercise what are commonly known as sacred functions, his ecclesiastical credentials. By what authority doest thou these things? they ask; And who gave thee this authority? In the other Christian communities the full proof of a man's ministry is looked for in the present rather than in the past. Can he and does he, as a matter of fact, convert souls from sin to righteousness? If he can and does, then let there be no minute investigation into pedigree, or captious search for title; but let the work authenticate the worker.

In the face of such divergencies as these, it would seem as if any attempt at reconciliation must bear failure written upon its face. The case looks still more hopeless when we remind ourselves that these contrasted estimates of the nature of the ministry have their roots deep down in that subsoil of human nature, which the ploughshare of logic does not so much as touch. The causes that make some men Nominalists and others Realists in philosophy, the causes that have made your neighbor a conservative and you a radical in politics, or *vice versa*, are resident in a region back of consciousness.

> " Out of darkness come the hands
> That reach through Nature, moulding man."

If therefore anybody imagines that it is in the power of council, conference, or synod to put forth an utterance potent to convert all the adherents of the institutional view to the successional idea, or all the adherents of the successional view to the institutional idea, I can simply answer that, for myself, I am under no such hallucination. I have no faith in any possible emulsion of oil and water; and while I admire the industry, I have small respect for the judgment of those sanguine mathematicians, who in their devotion to impossible tasks emulate Sisyphus and his rolling stone. I am contented to believe that parallel lines continued to infinity can never meet, transcendentalists to the contrary notwithstanding. And yet ideas that cannot be theoretically reconciled admit sometimes of practical adjustment. The *solvitur ambulando* principle applies to other problems than that of motion. The differences of opinion that divide men upon the subject of Church polity are really no wider than those that sunder them in the region of political philosophy. Engage a group of statesmen in a discussion of the principles of international law, provoke a club of political economists into a debate over the definition of wealth, propound at a social science congress the question of the true nature of punishment, and straightway almost as many judgments will emerge as there are brains working. Nevertheless, the nations for the most part live together in peace; wealth, whatever may be the true theory of it, is quietly amassed and securely held; and prison discipline is maintained. It is true, as I have already admitted, that behind our unity in these civil and social matters there lies the hidden arm of force, ready at any moment, as representing the convictions of the greater number, to pound us into unity if we attempt anything subversive of the established order. Yet, surely, Christians ought, sooner or later, to learn under the compulsion of love the lessons which citizens have to be taught by the compulsion of force.

At any rate the men of the Lambeth Conference of 1888 were sanguine enough to account such an improved state of things at least imaginable, even if not imminent or probable. Their utterance upon the subject of the ministry has been, as was naturally to be expected, more sharply criticised than any other portion of their platform. Some have seen in it an offensive assertion of prerogative ; others have interpreted it as an invitation to all men to turn Anglican without delay ; still others have been moved to ask, Who are these Bishops that they should venture thus to speak before they have been spoken to ? And yet these ministers of Christ in conference assembled could scarcely have used more carefully guarded language, supposing them to have felt it their duty to say anything at all upon the subject. All they did was to suggest a *modus vivendi.* Carefully avoiding the well-known phrase "Apostolical Succession," which would have committed them hopelessly to a particular philosophy of the ministry, and made the winning of those who hold to the institutional idea impossible, they fastened on certain words, the characteristic of which is, that they express a fact without at all insisting upon any theory of the fact. "The Historic Episcopate," they said, "locally adapted in the methods of its administration to the varying needs of the nations and peoples called of God into the unity of his Church." That government by oversight, which is what "episcopacy" when translated means, has been historically the prevailing method of polity in Christendom, certainly from the second century onwards, is beyond dispute. That associated with this episcopacy there has been a constant endeavor (whether successful or no, I am not now arguing) to maintain orderly succession, nobody denies. To what then does the Bishops' suggestion amount except to this, that if we are to have organic unity at all, it is more reasonable to expect that it should be brought about under this method of pilotage than under any other. There would seem to be nothing either unreasonable or arrogant in this. It is a simple falling back on fact. Think as you please, the Bishops seem to say, about the nature and the sanction of the Christian ministry. All we have to urge is that if a harmonious and self-consistent method of administering the word and the sacraments is the thing sought, the voice of human experience uttering itself through history suggests that a system of oversight safe-guarded by careful-ness in the transmission of authority is the more excellent way. Had the Bishops said, "Take our word for it, there has been no break anywhere in our dynasty;" had they said, "Be ye sure of this, that unless you company with us there is no grace in you," they would, indeed, as seekers after reconciliation, have made themselves a gazing-stock. But these are the things, be it observed, which they did not say.

If it be urged that there is a little interval of cloudi-ness between the New Testament days, when we see Christ appointing Apostles and St. Paul appointing deputies, and those not much later days, when by the acknowledgment of all historians the system of over-sight is found everywhere established throughout Christendom, the answer is, that however fatal this circumstance may be to alleged demonstrations of "apostolical succession," it does not lay so much as a feather's weight of opprobrium upon the argument for "the historic episcopate." As is well known, the authentic Christian literature of the times immediately subsequent to the Apostolic age, is not abundant. The Church grew noiselessly.

"The towers of Ilium like a mist arose."

The city of God came not with observation, and the builders were more careful to do their work than to leave records of the process. If, however, as soon as we come to the place where hints and vestiges begin to abound, we again find the method of appointment and commission as evidently the prevalent one, as we saw it to be in the days on the other side of the cloud, certainly the presumption, to use no stronger word, is in favor of the belief that what was historical before, and has been historical since, was also historical during that interval period upon which doubt has, in post-Reformation times, been cast. And yet a presumption, strong as it may be, cannot be made the basis of a proof; and the Bishops did that for which posterity will thank them, when they took the Historic Episcopate rather than the Apostolical Succession for the key-note of their appeal.

VI.

A CHURCH BY LOVE ESTABLISHED.

Politics are from God; not only allowing and approving governments, but commanding them, for the better manifestation of his own glory, and men's greater good, temporal and spiritual. Hence it is evident that POLITICS, both CIVIL and ECCLESIASTICAL, belong unto THEOLOGY, and are but a branch of the same. — GEORGE LAWSON.

Yes, by willing angels; by the Holy Ghost; by the inspired Word; by indestructible sacraments; by many instruments and intermediates; but chiefest of all by his own direct power in men both good and bad, in one inspiring and in the other restraining, — He triumphantly defends the Church and turns all her defeats into victories; putting her out among the instabilities of the world and the whirl of its mutations as one thing that cannot be shaken; overthrowing nations, but preserving her; rolling a tide here, in which empires, races, tongues, philosophies, arts, landmarks, codes, thrones, and every conceivable grandeur and fancied immortality are made to sink and disappear like foundered ships, while on this same tide, and over its peopled sepulchres, He causes this one indestructible to ride.

N. J. BURTON.

VI.

A CHURCH BY LOVE ESTABLISHED.

In commending to English-speaking Christendom a particular form of governance and ministry as most agreeable to past precedent taken in the large, the Bishops at Lambeth were careful to speak guardedly. Had they supplemented their mention of the Historic Episcopate with nothing more gracious than Pilate's peremptory " What I have written I have written," the utterance which they intended as an invitation would certainly have been construed as a demand. As men appreciative of contemporary fact, while not irreverent towards old tradition, they chose otherwise. Cheerfully tolerant of those lines of national diversity which they knew it to have been the constant endeavor of the papal policy to wipe out, they phrased their thought about governmental unity as follows : " *The Historic Episcopate, locally adapted in the methods of its administration to the varying needs of the nations and peoples called of God into the Unity of his Church.*"

Nothing could be more evident than the intention here to distinguish between what is permanent and what is variable in connection with the episcopal

14

regimen. We have already studied the essentials of
episcopacy, as such, and found them to be reducible
under the two heads of Christlikeness as respects the
exercise of a threefold function, and continuity, pre-
sumable even if not demonstrable, as respects the
tenure and transfer of authority. These central characteristics admit of no subtraction, they are of the
essence of the thing; but whatever is more than
these may count for surplusage.

Few Americans, for instance, a hundred years ago,
had any more adequate notion of a bishop's attributes
than was conveyed by the engraved portraits of eminent prelates of the Georgian period that, here or
there adorned the walls of some colonial governor or
Church-of-England townsman. The full-bottomed
wig and ample display of lawn that made the body
of the picture, together with the mitre and pastoral
staff skilfully worked in as marginal features of the
plate, were most impressive in their way; but the
savor was distinctly a savor of the things seen and
temporal. This disposition to look askance at episcopacy as being presumably first cousin to royalty,
was, of course, strongest in the States that had been
originally founded in the anti-prelatical interest; but
no doubt it was well-pronounced all along the coast.

It must be confessed that the solicitude of the
new democracy was not unnatural. Those were
Erastian days; and the very mention of episcopacy
carried with it thoughts of lions, unicorns, kings,
lords, and commons. As well might an ardent non-

juror of Sussex or Kent have tried to persuade the village squire at a parish dinner to make two separate toasts of Throne and Altar, as White or Seabury have labored to convince the Americans of their day, that episcopacy was not in some sense an appanage of the British Crown. How strongly this was felt by White himself is evident throughout his pamphlet. "*The Case of the Episcopal Churches in the United States Considered.*" In the Preface to this brochure he writes: "A prejudice has prevailed with many that the Episcopal Churches cannot otherwise exist than under the dominion of Great Britain. A Church Government that would contain the constituent principles would remove that anxiety which at present hangs over the Church of England, and yet be independent of foreign jurisdiction and influence on the minds of many sincere persons." The very fact that it had been found necessary to expurgate the Prayer-book in order to banish the Royal Family from the thoughts of the worshipping congregation, was of itself *prima facie* evidence that episcopacy ought to be reckoned as part and parcel of the old order of things now put away for ever. Moreover, were there not here and there in parishes, all the way from Portsmouth to Savannah, glebes, parsonages, Queen Anne Bibles and communion plate, and other visible possessions, the legal title to which had, since the surrender at Yorktown, rested solely upon the understanding that the body claiming them as its property was historically and actually the successor and

legatee of the organization before known as The
Church of England in the Colonies? And yet, in
spite of all the prejudices, convictions, and associations thus engendered, no intelligent American to-
day considers that there is any necessary connection
between a bishop, a full-bottomed wig, and a seat in
the House of Lords. We have learned something,
and are learning more. We perceive that the distinction between the transient and the permanent, so
valuable in our studies of all things else, has value
also in the criticism of episcopacy. It is evident that
the acceptance by a people of this particular polity
does not necessarily involve a reception of all the
concomitants that in the mind of another people
may have been wrapped up with it.

An interesting question now presents itself. In the
case of the nation to which we ourselves by birth or
by adoption belong, what are the special "needs" to
which, in the "methods of its administration" the
Historic Episcopate might fairly be expected to
"adapt" itself? Here is this American people "called
of God into the unity of his Church," how shall the
Historic Episcopate mould itself into harmony with
the race instincts it here encounters?

There is, of course, a base and unworthy sense in
which this notion of adaptation may be entertained;
with that we have nothing to do. Any modification
of polity that should involve the lowering by a hair's
breadth of the standard of holiness whether for priests
or people would be fatal. There are American char-

acteristics to which the Historic Episcopate could never adapt itself without playing traitor to the Bishop of bishops, the Shepherd of all souls.

But what are the great structural principles of social life to which this nation, as a nation, stands committed? What maxims with respect to governance and polity and organization have become such current coin among us as to seem axiomatic? Accurately to distinguish these *Americana* will be to take a long step towards understanding what, in our own case at least, the Lambeth language means.

Prominent among the better characteristics of our national mind stands reverence for what is constitutional, as contrasted with what is arbitrary, in the exercise of power. This trait came to us with our English blood, having been perhaps intensified by a century of life under a written constitution. Not that there is any special efficacy in written constitutions which unwritten ones may not and do not share; only it will scarcely be denied that the embodiment of great constitutional principles in actual terms, known and read of all men, does tend to concentrate, and by concentrating to intensify, a people's reverence for its organic law. The document becomes the visible symbol of that peculiar combination of thoughts and feelings which gives a nation its personal identity, and is cherished accordingly. The Count de Maistre, a profound thinker on this subject, in his dislike for whatever he suspects of having been extemporized, goes the length of denying that there was or ever can be any such thing as a written constitution in the true sense of the word.[1] Had he lived to see the centenary of the Constitution of the United States, he might possibly have modified the harshness of his utterances upon this point. He was fond of buttressing his statements with citations from Holy Scripture, and, had he looked, he might have found a precedent for written constitutions as far back as the days of the Judges. "Then Samuel," the record runs, "told the people the manner of the kingdom, and wrote it in a book, and laid it up before the Lord." And yet, no doubt, the material out of which Samuel made his book was constitutional material; there was precedent, more or less abundant, for the "manner of the kingdom;" and De Maistre must be allowed to be right, at least so far as this, that when wise men write constitutions they never do it off-hand and *de novo*, but only seek to put into words things already found by experience to be true.

The great value of a constitution, whether written or only traditional, lies in its efficacy as a barrier against despotism. This is what it means for a monarchy to be "limited;" the thing that limits is the constitution, which imposes on the kingdom its "manner" or fixed form, to wit, the boundary lines that may not be overstepped. We are accustomed to speak of the United States as being that phenomenal thing, a na-

[1] Essai sur le Principe Générateur des Constitutions Politiques, § ix.

tion "born in a day," and we pride ourselves on being able to name the day; but this is questionable talk. The blossom of the century plant, when at last it bursts, has all the suddenness of a miracle; but only the patient absorption of much now forgotten sunshine has made the flowering possible. The Constitution of the United States was not created instantaneously out of nothing. Genius had much to do with it, but Divine Providence had more. Its very first paragraph presupposes a knowledge of antecedent facts. The Pentecost rather than the Fourth of July is the day that ought to be honored as the real birth-day of what we now know as civil liberty. It was then, to speak accurately, that Christendom began to be. For is it not clear that only by such a general diffusion of right-mindedness as Christ's religion has brought to pass, can government of a people by laws of its own making, and rulers of its own choosing, be possible? Just in proportion as God pours out His spirit on all flesh, can all flesh be trusted to walk alone. The old attempts at free government perished, "having not the Spirit." Even Samuel's limited monarchy came to naught. But for a world baptized with the Holy Ghost, better things are possible. Government of the many by the few is necessary when the many are in the dark, and only the few have light; but when the many get the light, then government by the few becomes an anachronism, the hour for self-government has struck. The de-Christianized race or nation loses this self-governing faculty; and that is the very peril which is confronting us to-day. The human body, as St. Paul so clearly discerned, is the only adequate emblem or parable of the perfect social state, and the human body, as we know, is governed in all its motions by a pervasive indwelling spirit. The power that opens or shuts the hand is a power transmitted along threads of communication which are hidden, and it asserts itself from within. When the crutch and the splint are brought into use, it is instantly perceived by observers that something has gone wrong. Hurt of one sort or another must have befallen the man, we say, or these outward assistances would not have been needed. The healthy body has all the essential mechanism of motion within itself. This is the image of the thoroughly Christianized community, every member of which speaks and acts as he is moved to do by the spirit of God uttering itself in and through the conscience. That we are far enough from this ideal condition, I need not waste breath in showing, but that this is the only working hypothesis upon which a democracy can hope to enjoy permanence is a point which Christian teachers ought to emphasize more strenuously than they do.

Now the constitution of the Church — I mean the entire Church, "Holy Church throughout all the world" — is an unwritten body of practical maxims which have accumulated under the teaching of the Spirit. There is, as we know, electricity in action, and again there is electricity stored, put away in reserve for use when needed; there is light in action, and again there is light garnered and laid up in the veins of coal. So with the spirit of wisdom, for the Spirit of God is the spirit of wisdom, — this also admits of accumulation ; this also may be put away in store, secreted. Thus the constitution of any given State — and the same can be said of the constitution of any national Church — is simply so much accumulated wisdom as it may have been given to that State or to that Church to discern and to embody. The constitution is to the government, whether civil or ecclesiastical, precisely what the balance-wheel is to the watch ; it secures the administration of affairs upon settled principles, rather than by freak or whim or passing impulse. If America and England deserve to be called the freest countries of the earth, it is because they, more consistently and more thoroughly than any of their sister nations, have carried out and embodied this conception of what government ought to be. This Anglo-American ideal stands forth the most clearly when we contrast it with absolutism on the one hand, and with out-and-out democracy on the other. Under absolutism, the ruler is supposed to hold a deposit of power directly intrusted to him by the Almighty, and what he says is law ; under democracy pure and simple, the voice of the people is alleged to be the only authentic voice of God, and though it shout one thing to-day and the contradictory of it to-morrow, it must be accepted as God's voice all the same. But under a free government, properly so-called, the voice of the people is accepted as the trustworthy index of the divine mind only in so far as it may be found upon examination to be in harmony with the great sum total of accumulated wisdom into possession of which the children of men have, through the experience of many generations, been gradually brought. This laboriously earned increment of wisdom is what makes a constitution. Doubtless, that is the supremely-favored society in which " the common sense of most " avails to hold in check the inevitable irrationality and waywardness of some; only in defining and determining our " most," we must be very careful not to be misled by merely temporary majorities ascertained by cast of ballot, count of heads, or show of hands, but to look rather to that great multitude of the wise and good of all times, times present and times past, whose judgment on the points at issue stands recorded.

In view of the profound attachment entertained for these principles by the American people, it is plain that no episcopate how historical soever will be likely to commend itself to them as having been locally adapted in the methods of its administration to their own particular need, unless it be a constitutional episcopate.

This is the secret of the deep distrust entertained by many, of the unitive schemes urged by the lovable and saintly Muhlenberg and his associates, in the so-called " Memorial Movement" of forty years ago. The plan was for the Bishops of the Protestant Episcopal Church to go forward on their own responsibility, and quite independently of any powers conferred on them in terms at their consecration, to ordain ministers of the Gospel who should serve wholly on the outside of Anglican lines. But it was felt, and I venture to think rightly felt, by the greater number, that however desirable it might be for the Episcopal Church to come into closer communication with those beyond its pale, it could not be right for any Bishop who had taken upon his lips the words, " In the name of God, Amen, I, N ———, do promise conformity and obedience to the doctrine, discipline, and worship of the Protestant Episcopal Church in the United States of America," — that it could not be right, I say, for any Bishop, so pledged and sworn, to perform acts of which neither the Constitution nor the Ordinal of the Church whose Bishop he was, made any mention. To the working of a constitutional episcopate it is essential that Bishops speak and act constitutionally.

We shall return by and by to this question of the connection between constitutional methods and eirenic plans; but, meanwhile, I note a second governmental principle as one to which the American mind is indissolubly wedded, namely, legislation by representation in contrast with legislation by edict. As the constitutional principle is the guarantee that power, whether legislative, judicial, or executive, shall not be arbitrarily employed regardless of the common understanding, either tacitly maintained or else registered in some great charter, so the representative principle is our guarantee that the current laws of the land shall be the expression of the people's will and bear the stamp of their assent. Here, as before, the Christian religion enters in as the controlling factor in the problem. How is it conceivable that any people can safely be entrusted with the making of its own laws, except it be a people in whose heart are God's ways? Just as really, therefore, may it be said of representative as of constitutional government, that without a doctrine of the Spirit it is futile. At any rate, whatever may be thought of the application of this doctrine to the State, there ought to be no doubt of our duty to recognize its workings in the Church. Certainly to the body of believers, if not to the Commonwealth, the Pentecostal promise runs that the law from having been an imposition from without shall become an utterance from within. It is this reversal of the point of view that really makes the difference between the two Testaments, and it was upon this issue that Moses, man of God, went out of the world's premiership, and Jesus, Son of God, came in. This is the democracy of the *Magnificat*, and the only democracy that can stand. To this idea of law-making by fairly elected representatives, the Anglo-American mind is knitted by tendons that bleed if you cut them, and no episcopate that should seek to waive or to nullify this feature of our social life could for a moment allege with any show of reason that it had been locally adapted in the methods of its administration to the needs of the people of the United States.

And here I bid you note the encouraging fact, that
with respect to the desirability of law-making by representation, American Christendom, with the exception
of the Roman Catholic portion of it, is already prac-
tically at one. Churches organized on the principle
of independency cannot of course permit the exercise
of legislative power by any body larger than the local
congregation ; though even these have their councils
and conferences, membership of which is conferred by
the representative method. But when it comes to the
case of those denominations that aim at organizing
themselves on national lines, it is safe to say that
the difference of principle involved in their respective
methods of legislation is so slight as to be inappre-
ciable. Save for a few catch-words of no importance
worth the mentioning, a man with his eyes shut would
scarcely know whether he was in the Presbyterian
General Assembly, the Methodist General Conference,
or the Episcopal General Convention. What does it
matter whether a measure pending in a deliberative
body be called a " canon " or an " overture " ? It is
substantially the same thing in both cases, namely,
an attempt to give shape to what is believed to be
the popular will, by the representative method. It is
true that in one of the bodies I just mentioned, — the
Episcopal General Convention, — the law-making has
to be done by what is known as the concurrent action
of two houses, each of which has a power of veto
upon the decisions of the other ; but this, instead of
making it the less American, only makes it the more

so; for legislation by single chamber has never found favor in this country, but, on the contrary, our civil laws, both State and Federal, have to run the gauntlet of two sets of critics before they can be engrossed. For ecclesiastical purposes either "council" or "synod" is a far better word than "convention," which to the American sense smacks of a political flavor; and it is pleasant to think how entirely at home in the popular branch of the national synod or council of "The United Church of the United States" we should all find ourselves.

A third American characteristic is fondness for a strong executive, when this may be had without any sacrifice of the guarantees of constitutional and legislative freedom. Our people almost worship efficiency. They like the man who in times of dimness and difficulty can say, I take the responsibility. In this regard episcopacy needs no adaptation; it is adapted already, and it is this very characteristic that to-day is commending it to the American mind. Fatherhood and leadership make the very essence of episcopacy, and in the task of prosecuting spiritual conquests, winning a people for God, fatherhood and leadership are what are needed most. The father's love and wisdom, the leader's clear-sightedness and dash, — what missionary qualifications are there that compare with these? In fact, is it not true that every denomination of Christians has already, in one shape or another, an episcopate of its own? Is there one among them all that does not look with more or less of deference to its leading spirits, its controlling minds? So true is this, that the late Dean of Westminster with characteristic ingenuity proposed that the argument for episcopacy should be shifted from sacerdotal grounds altogether, and made to rest on the well-established sociological fact that power of leadership is the inheritance of only a certain percentage of human kind.

With St. Paul to back me in my choice of words, I cannot think that I shall seem to you to be lowering the subject, if, while dwelling upon this phase of it, I call attention to the way in which efficiency is secured in handicrafts. In the familiar titles "foreman," "journeyman" and "apprentice," do we not see reflected Bishop, Priest, and Deacon? And is it not true that such a partitioning of functions, such a distribution of effort, lies bedded in the very nature of things, quite apart from all question of apostolical precedent and canonical usage? Contractor, carpenter, helper,— can you build your house without these? Yes, perhaps, after a fashion; but in house-building on a large scale it is wise to allow for the employment of all these. It is a homely illustration, I grant you, of the truth that a three-fold cord is not quickly broken, but then we must remember that the highest verities and the humblest often lie close together. The parables of our Lord are in the same condemnation, if condemnation it be.

The Hegelian philosophy of the Trinity finds strength in the fact that it makes appeal to the familiar data of consciousness, and it may be that my work-a-day argu-

ment for Bishops, Priests, and Deacons may not prove
the less persuasive for having been based upon the
experience of common life. Efficiency is intrinsically
a homely theme, and must needs draw its illustrations from the prosaic side of life; but then we have
to remember that Martha's place in the one household of God is as real and as necessary as Mary's.
The ministers of Christ are servers always, and of
servers it is required that they be found efficient.

Another principle very precious to the Anglo-
American mind is that of the maintenance of organic unity by what is known as the federal method,
— the combination, that is to say, of the two ideas of
sovereignty and of what has been happily called "sub-
sovereignty;" the sovereignty being resident in the
Union, and the sub-sovereignty in the States. Here
again we shall discover that episcopacy suffers no violence by adaptation, but, on the contrary, lends itself
with cheerful readiness to meet what is required of it.
For, when we think of it, every rightly-ordered community is a union of householders, each of which has
its head. Just as the molecule is the unit of crystalline
structure and the cell the unit of vegetable structure, so
is the family the unit of social structure. The aggregate may be larger or smaller, so small perhaps as to
be called a tribe, so large as to be called a nation; but,
whether tribe or nation, when analyzed it is found to
be made up of families, each one of which, while conceding sovereignty to the aggregate, retains meanwhile
a sub-sovereignty proper to itself, each father being

the head of his own household. In ecclesiastical sociology, what would seem to answer best to this relation between the family and the aggregate of families? Most evidently a like relation between the group that clusters itself about one spiritual leader who answers to the father, and the aggregate of such groups. If now for leader or father, we read bishop; and for aggregate, read national Church, have we not the very thing that corresponds perfectly with the American conception of organic unity through federalism?

I should like to pause here and dwell upon the highly suggestive and sympathetic bearing of all this on the ecclesiastical system known as Congregationalism, or, in its still more elementary form, as Independency. The great truth embedded in Independency, and it cannot be too strongly emphasized, is the sacredness of the ecclesiastical unit, and the insistence that this unit shall be maintained by a personal bond, an actual tie knitting the teacher to the taught. Independency insists that without the molecule there can be no crystal, without the cell no body; and if in its zeal in this direction it has suffered the crystal and the body themselves to fall out of mind and be forgotten, we ought not for that reason to be indifferent to the value of the lesson which the story of Congregationalism in America, and especially in New England, teaches. The Massachusetts and Connecticut parish of early eighteenth-century days, conterminous as it was with the township, and so

15

ordered that the whole population, men, women, and children, came under the spiritual headship and guidance of one pastor, was probably the best illustration of the ideal of what I have called the ecclesiastical unit, that Christianity in this country has ever seen. Assuredly no bishop of Anglican lineage has ever, on this side of the ocean, exercised a territorial episcopate (understanding the word for the moment in its simple sense of spiritual oversight) that could compare for general acceptance with the unchallenged rule of an Edwards or a Davenport. That Congregationalism even on its own chosen ground should have failed to maintain its standing order, is a fact for which those who account the system an imperfect and one-sided one, have of course their own explanation. Upon this phase of the subject it would be ungracious to dwell; my main purpose in referring to Independency at all having been my wish to bear testimony to the unspeakable value of the principle by which it has ever set such store; namely, the truth that the rudimentary unit of the visible body of Christ is the group of souls clustered about one personal centre, himself father or shepherd according as we account his group to be " family " or " flock."

Whatever bright prospects may be beckoning forward the Episcopal Church in the United States, of one thing we may be sure, that if this primeval truth concerning the unit is forgotten, there is nothing but disaster in store. No aggrandizement of the diocese can possibly make up for the loss of the personal tie that ought to link a shepherd of souls to every separate soul in the flock over which the Holy Ghost may have made him overseer. Should God grant this unity movement success upon a large scale, the number of souls to be cared for would be so great that bishoprics would shrink to very modest territorial limits indeed In that event Counties might become Dioceses, and States Provinces, — a reversion in one respect to the well-known purpose of the organizers of the American Episcopal Church, who were ever solicitous to observe State lines. Under such an arrangement, the organization of the Church would answer to the organization of the Country almost as face to face, the aggregates of the ecclesiastical units corresponding to the aggregates of civil units perfectly.

But what of the difficulty at the other end of the line? When it comes to the matter of aggregating our ecclesiastical units, where, some one may very naturally ask, are we to stop? What logical landing-place is there short of the seven hills where Leo sits? Why should the Christian Church, spiritual corporation that it is, take any notice of civil boundary lines, which, as we know, are here to-day and there to-morrow? Would it not be better to accept the principle of œcumenicity as the Roman Church presents it to us, and consent to merge all our units in the one great Latin union which is so ready to receive and to absorb them? This raises a point so interesting that we cannot but wish to consider it, so crucial that we have no right to shun it. The

philosophy of national churches, the whole question of
their genesis and their right to be, is a matter that
greatly needs clearing up. As everybody knows, they
are the *bête noire* of Rome. It was the national character of the English Church that made it what, before
these Tractarian days, good Anglicans delighted to
call it, " the bulwark of the Reformation." To fight
a nation up in arms for what it believed to be its spiritual liberties was found even by a world-monarch no
laughing matter.

But why, if we admit the desirability of any aggregation of local churches, is not Rome right in
the contention ? Why is not her inviting catholicity a better and truer thing than our eagerly
sought, and as yet confessedly not found nationality ? National Churches, I answer, find their sanction
and warrant in these words of Jesus Christ, " My
kingdom is not of this world; if my kingdom were of
this world, then would my servants fight." Rome
has misconceived this sentence as seriously as ever
Pilate did. Its true import is to this effect, that
since Christ's kingdom is a spiritual organism it
cannot push itself by material methods, but, so far
as localization and delimitation are concerned, must
conform itself to such boundary lines as the civil
power for its own purposes may have drawn. The
State is the great force-organization, the Church is
the great love-organization, and the moment the love-
organization begins to say, " I insist that the territory
shall be divided thus and so," that moment it usurps

the functions of the force-organization, discredits its own title of "kingdom of heaven," and lapses into worldliness. The papal theologians are fond of seeing in the two swords the disciples in the Garden of Gethsemane offered Christ, a symbol of the combined temporal and spiritual authorities; but it is more natural to infer from our Lord's words, "It is enough," that his purpose was to disavow swords altogether. "What have I to do with weapons such as these?" He seems to say; and his healing of the hurt of Malchus on the spot points to the same conclusion. For that kind of work, He would have them understand, He was not responsible; his servants had misunderstood Him. How they have gone on misunderstanding Him through all the so-called Christian ages, we know only too well. The true answer, therefore, to Rome's demand that there shall be a world-wide visible Church is this, — Your motive is good, but your endeavor is premature. Œcumenicity is of itself a most desirable thing; but you are in too great a hurry to catholicize the world. The love-organization cannot hope to be visibly unified over the whole globe, until the force-organization shall first so have unified itself. Hear what St. Paul saith, "That is not first which is spiritual, but that which is natural, and afterward that which is spiritual." This is as true of the ecclesiastical as it is of the human organism. Our aggregate of units can be no larger than civil government will let it be. We Christians desire to see the aggregates become as large as may be, and we should hail with joy that advent of the "parliament of man" which would make œcumenicity possible; but, for the present, the national church is the largest union attainable, and with this we must rest content. There being no united world there can be no united church of that dimension; but no such moral impossibility forbids our hope of a United Church of the United States, for the course of this nation has happily been peaceably ordered by God's governance, that it ought to be possible here for his Church to serve Him "in all godly quietness," which is but another name for unity. This is our answer to Rome, and it is a sufficient answer.

We come back to the point from which we started, namely, the feasibility of unifying American Christianity by the method known as consolidation. In the light of all that has been said, what practical measures would seem to be possible? One resort is ever open to us, and perhaps, in the immediate present, only one, "Men ought always to pray." Nor do we need, for that matter, to frame any new or untried supplication; "Thy kingdom come," covers it all. But how may we best follow up our prayer? We are American Christians, with certain grave responsibilities resting on us in virtue of our being Americans rather than Latins or Orientals; what may we do to make possible that concerted action on the part of God's people in this land, the lack of which entails such scandal? This much, at least, to start with, — We may recognize the fact that the material for the

United Church of the United States is ready to our hand in the persons of all those who by whatever hand have been baptized into the Name of the Father, the Son, and the Holy Ghost. These constitute that Church *in posse* which we would see become the Church *in esse*. These make the citizenship of the Kingdom. But how may the existing organizations help the movement on? Here are these ten or twelve great churches; what can they severally do to bring to pass the one still greater Church? I cannot without presumption venture upon offering counsel to any save that single one of the too numerous group to which I am personally attached. To her, as her loyal minister, I have a perfect right to speak, so that I do it modestly and out of an honest heart, no matter how little the thing said may deserve to engage her thought.

My belief is that the Episcopal Church may best help forward the movement we have been studying, by a gradual and tentative moulding of her present Constitution into a closer conformity with the principles formally enunciated at Lambeth. This statement of essentials, although never given the force of statute law by binding enactment, has, nevertheless, met with such complete acquiescence on the part of the clergy and people of the Anglican Communion throughout the world, that it may almost be said to have been adopted by general consent. What now would it mean to conform the written Constitution of the American Episcopal Church to the principles of the

Lambeth platform? This one thing it would mean if no more; the doing so would be the best possible evidence of our sincerity and good faith in putting forward the proposal in question. Some may think that to let this consideration sway us would be a compromise of our self-respect, — a sort of acknowledgment that others had had a right to suspect us of shamming. But if our chief solicitude in this matter be to preserve our dignity intact, we shall accomplish little. The question is, Have not others a perfect right to expect that, after having said we would unite with them on certain terms, we should go on and provide some method of making the acceptance of the terms a practicable thing? There is no such method, nor can there be, unless by way of constitutional enactment. Again I throw out the caution, Let us shun the rock on which the Memorial Movement split. Let all things be done in order. Since the year 1789 the Constitution of the American Episcopal Church has been amended fourteen times. No proposal still further to amend it can therefore properly be stigmatized as presumptuous or unprecedented.

One great improvement, entirely in the line of the Lambeth proposals, would be to place at the very beginning of the instrument the confession of our faith.[1] Surely the constitution of a Church is the natural place to look when one is seeking to find out

[1] The Council of Trent set a good example in this respect, if in no other. In the forefront of its dogmatic utterances it places the Nicene Creed.

what such Church considers fundamental to her very being. But what do we find greeting us at the threshold of the Constitution of the American Episcopal Church? We find certain provisions regulating the time and place for the meeting of the General Convention, and specifying what shall be done in case of the breaking out of an epidemic disease in the town or city previously designated for such meeting. This is lamentably, and but for the seriousness of the subject, I should say, ludicrously inadequate. Doubtless, what prevented the framers of the Constitution from putting anything doctrinal into the first article of that instrument was the sense of a certain ill-defined duty of allegiance to the Thirty-nine Articles of the Church of England. They failed to perceive, and considering the novelty of the situation we cannot wonder at it, — that, in drawing up a written constitution for a new national Church, they were doing a thing that ought to work the supersession of the Thirty-nine Articles altogether.[1] They were undertaking to do for the Church what the members of the Constitutional Convention, about the

[1] So long ago as 1782, Bishop, then Doctor, White wrote as follows with respect to the status of the Thirty-nine Articles : " For the doctrinal part, it would perhaps be sufficient to demand of all admitted to the ministry, or engaged in ecclesiastical legislation, the questions contained in the Book of Ordination, which extends no further than an acknowledgment of the Scriptures as a rule of faith and life ; yet some general sanction may be given to the Thirty-nine Articles, so as to adopt their leading sense, which is here proposed rather as a chain of union, than for exacting entire uniformity of sentiment." (The Case of the Episcopal Churches in the United States considered, p.13).

same time, did for the State, — namely, to put in writing the organic law. Their duty with respect to the Thirty-nine Articles, then as now a part of the organic law of the Church of England, was to incorporate into the new Constitution of the Church so much of their substance as they held to be essential, and to let the rest drop. Instead of doing this, they allowed the question of the true status of the Articles to drag along in an indeterminate way until the year 1801, when at last a formal recognition was accorded them. But it must be confessed that ever since their transfer from English to American soil, the Thirty-nine Articles have had a provisional and transitory look. One of them has a title with nothing after it. To another a saving clause has been added, to warn readers of the Second Book of Homilies against certain references therein contained to the constitution and laws of England. Surely it can never have been imagined that of such sort would be the permanent dogmatic constitution of a great Church. Why not look facts in the face? The Thirty-nine Articles were originally drawn up by the English Church as a defence against the Rome of the sixteenth century. Rome having, deliberately changed her base in the year of our Lord 1870, does not our elaborate battery look, to the critical eye of present-day strategists, a little out of range? Would not the embodiment in the first Article of our Constitution of what the Bishops at Lambeth laid down with respect to the Scriptures and the Creeds, completely meet our needs? In fact, upon any hy-

pothesis of consolidation, are we not in honor and
in duty bound, if we propose to stand by what these
Bishops said, to make this very adaptation? It may be
that the time will come when the Thirty-nine Articles,
bound up with the Westminster Confession (not thrown
aside, but laid aside), will be given a place of honorary
retirement among the theological archives of the English-speaking peoples. To disown these old confessions
would be for the great communions with whose history
they are respectively associated an act of deep ingrati-
tude; to disuse them might be an act of discriminating
wisdom.

One other, and only one other, constitutional
point needs mentioning, and that is the matter of
worship. Probably no single feature of the unity
movement has occasioned more disquietude to conservative minds in the Episcopal Church than the
absence from the Lambeth platform of any saving-
clause with respect to a prescribed form of worship.
Except as respects the actual words of institution in
the case of the two sacraments, the silence of the platform upon the subject of devotional formularies is complete. But does this mean that the favorers of unity
upon the Lambeth lines desire to alter by so much as
a letter the Book of Common Prayer, or to abridge in
the slightest degree the privileges of those to whom
the aroma of its devotions is as the breath of life?
Certainly not. Perhaps no greater calamity could
befall either English or American religion than would
be involved in the disappearance of that particular

type of Christian character which a loyal and faithful use of the Book of Common Prayer engenders. The really desirable thing is, not the destruction, but the conservation of any and all types that are good. But what is to hinder that within the pale of a consolidated Church various methods of worship should be in use side by side — at least, until by general consent, and in virtue of the law of the survival of the fittest, one or another of them had come to be recognized as the more excellent way? A practical method of constitutionally carrying out this inclusive policy would be the one already suggested, namely, that of classifying local churches under such titles as Congregations of the Anglican Rite, worshipping in accordance with the Book of Common Prayer; Congregations of the German Rite, worshipping in accordance with what are at present known as Lutheran forms; and Congregations of the Puritan rite, worshipping without any liturgy at all, except in so far as the sacramental words of institution may be said of themselves to make a liturgy. This would not be absolute uniformity, I grant; but is anybody expecting absolute uniformity? Is anybody desiring it? To reduce the competing houses of worship in our country villages even to three, would be a distinct gain; and with constitutional provision made for " high ritual," " low ritual" and "no ritual," such a reduction ought, in a United Church of the United States, to become possible. In that event no Episcopalian need lose what is most precious to him; nor any Presbyterian, Congregationalist, or Methodist suffer forfeiture of those precious associations that in his mind are indissolubly linked to what he accounts the simpler method of approaching the throne of God. Meanwhile, the whole village would be the stronger for knowing that one communion held both the Anglican and the Covenanter in its embrace, — nothing having been lost, much having been gained.

It will be said that the country is not prepared for this. Nothing could be truer. The question is, — Could we be better employed than in furthering the needed preparation? That a desired consummation is a hundred years away, ought not to discourage brave men from breaking ground and beginning the approach; and at any rate

> "It never yet did hurt
> To lay down likelihoods and forms of hope."

Of course, if one is persuaded that nothing in the present state of things needs mending, his strength is to sit still. But it is difficult to understand how such a longing for a more perfect union, as evidently is in the minds of many, should have arisen without cause. So woe-begone and pitiful to some of us does the present broken, nay splintered, condition of contemporary Christendom appear, that, as believers in the divine origin of our religion, we cannot but seem to ourselves to be shut up to one or other of two conclusions, — either that Almighty God is bent on bringing to pass, through all this disintegration, a better and truer unity than has ever been before; or else that what we see going on before our eyes is the slow merging of the ecclesiastical in the civil order,— the coming in of the so-called "gospel of the secular life," the practical obliteration of the Church, as of an institution that has fulfilled its mission for the sanctifying of society. For this latter alternative, in the face of a whole world lying in wickedness, we are not prepared; therefore, we take the former. This drives us into building-projects whether we will or no; hence, if we vex you by our importunity, try to think of us as of men upon whom a necessity is laid; if we seem the victims of "a craze," try to remember that so Paul looked to Festus, and Simon Peter to those who on the day of Pentecost thought him "full of new wine."

To those of his Anglo-Catholic friends who with indecent haste are for burying the Lambeth Platform out of sight as a dead failure, because it has not brought Christendom into unity within the space of four years, the writer would commend one of George Herbert's *Jacula Prudentum*, "Evening words are not like to morning."

But, if build we must, only one point has to be decided. On what lines and according to what dimensions ought our edification to proceed?

There are two perspective drawings of the Church of Christ often hung up for us to look at and admire, but neither of which, I venture to insist, deserves our unqualified approval. One is a dreamy, Turneresque representation of a building, large enough to be sure, and lofty enough, but so completely wrapped about with wreaths of mist, that we are left very much in the dark as to what the structure is; we cannot tell where it begins or where it ends. The thought of the architect is hopelessly concealed by the water-colorist's too generous fog; the whole thing is a suggestion, nothing more. The other picture represents a tidy little building, snug and compact, jauntily balanced upon a narrow ledge of rock. There is no mystery about it at all. We see the whole thing at a glance. It evidently will not accommodate many people; but then, nobody can deny that the outline is faultless, the symbolism correct, and the masonry beyond reproach. There is no mist in the air, there are no clouds in the sky; the whole thing is distinct, well-defined, pretty to look at, small.

The one picture is from the hand of the liberalist, the other from the hand of the sectarian, — Anglican, sectarian, or another, it matters not. The former of them gives us largeness without definiteness; its companion, definiteness without size.

In our endeavors at unifying the national religion and helping forward the People's Church, it will be wise of us to take neither of these architectural attempts for our accepted model, but rather to aim at such lines of structure as shall impress themselves on all observers as being alike generous and clean-cut.

THE END.